Y0-BSE-663

TRUTHS TO LIVE BY

TRUTHS TO LIVE BY

BY
JOHN ELLIOTT ROSS

Essay Index Reprint Series

Originally Published by
HENRY HOLT AND COMPANY
NEW YORK

BOOKS FOR LIBRARIES PRESS
FREEPORT, NEW YORK

Library of Congress Cataloging in Publication Data

Ross, John Elliot, 1884-1946.
  Truths to live by.

  (Essay index reprint series)
  1. Apologetics--20th century. I. Title.
BT1101.R78 1972   239'.7   72-37834
ISBN 0-8369-2622-6

PRINTED IN THE UNITED STATES OF AMERICA
BY
NEW WORLD BOOK MANUFACTURING CO., INC.
HALLANDALE, FLORIDA 33009

INTRODUCTION

I AM by temperament and by training a Protestant. But it is not unfitting, I think, that I should write this introductory word to a book by a distinguished priest of the great Catholic communion, for it is with the spiritual dilemmas of my generation that he deals in clarity and candor.

We are children of an age that has grown lean on its alternate diets of sentimental metaphysics and sterile negations. And in our spiritual poverty we hunger for more profound satisfactions than we have found either in logic or in the laboratory.

We are not as blasé as we seem. Behind our varied poses of unconcern is an ineradicable interest in the mystery and mastery of life. We want, more than all else, light on the mystery of life and leadership in the mastery of life.

Several years ago Christopher Morley wrote a beguiling tale with the beguiling title of *Where the Blue Begins*. It was the story of the spiritual adventures of Gissing, a dog Morley invested with human passions and human perplexities.

[iii]

INTRODUCTION

Gissing's dog-soul was harassed by the inscrutable issues of life and destiny, and, like most of us, he was driven by a hunger for "a horizon that would stay blue when he reached it." Gissing's greatest hunt was for God. With his dog-nose, as sensitive as a poet's spirit, Gissing tirelessly sought to scent the footsteps of God through the mire and maze of human affairs, in cathedral and counting-house, on land and sea, towards some horizon that would prove immortally blue. Here are some things Morley said of Gissing's research magnificent.

"The very solitude that Gissing craved and revelled in was, by a sublime paradox, haunted by a mysterious loneliness. He felt sometimes as though his heart had been broken off from some great whole, to which it yearned to be reunited. It felt like a bone that had been buried, which God would some day dig up. . . . People who have had an arm or leg amputated, Gissing reflected, say that they can still feel pains in the absent member. Well, there's an analogy in that. Modern skepticism has amputated God from the heart; but there is still a twinge where the arteries were sewn up." I think Gissing is a good symbol of the malady and mood of this generation.

[iv]

INTRODUCTION

I find myself very much at sea between the Scylla of Fundamentalism and the Charybdis of Modernism. As I have said elsewhere, I am left cold alike by the unsound affirmations of dialectical Fundamentalists and by the sound negations of argumentative Modernists. In the light of many intellectual considerations, I find myself drawn irresistibly into the camp of religious liberalism. And yet there is in me some dim desire that will hold me fascinated at a street-corner listening to the exhortations of an illiterate street preacher, despite my inner revolt against what seem to me his inadequate and ignorantly naïve conceptions of life and destiny. I suspect that this is something more than a laggard emotionalism that intelligence has failed completely to rout. I suspect I am but echoing the hunger of my generation for an energizing faith that will, as Kirsopp Lake puts it, satisfy the soul of the saint without disgusting the intellect of the scholar. I am neither a saint nor a scholar, but I have this hunger because I belong to a generation that is perplexed by this dilemma. Like Gissing, this generation is hungry for a sense of union with "some great whole" from which it feels broken off and for a God who "is something more than a formula on Sunday and an oath during the week."

The more I delve into the lives of the great spirits from whom the decisive epochs in the history of science and the history of religion have taken their names, the more I am impressed by the fact that the great scientist and the great mystic have much in common. Both are venturesome pioneers. Both walk with a sublime faith into the unknown that lies beyond the white light of the known that falls about their feet. Both are seeking a deeper reality than meets the eye. And this gives me hope that mankind may one day heal the breach between science and religion, may one day close the gulf that has been thrown between reason and faith by the short-sighted.

To the end of time mankind will be seeking to discover the living significance of religion. And, as now, a thousand roads will be tramped over in the quest. Men approach the issues of life and destiny along different roads. It is important that men who **have** walked these roads shall tell why they chose them and what they found on their way. And it is important that we listen to the tale of their travels. If the telling and the hearing are to bring light and leadership to a perplexed and hungry generation, two things are necessary. Those who speak must be free alike from the sins of flippancy and of fanaticism. And those who listen must be free alike from the prejudgments of blind credulity and of blind cynicism.

In this book, Father Ross has lived up to his half of such a bargain. He is neither flippant with the faithless nor fanatic in the statement of his faith. Here is no plea for blind credulity. However widely I find myself differing from Father Ross at this point or that, throughout this book I have the sense of listening to one who is deeply concerned with the intrinsic rather than the incidental aspects of religion. This book is not simply an argumentative treatise. It is the report of a religious pilgrim who has travelled an ancient highway in his quest of spiritual satisfaction and who, on that highway, has, for himself, found faith reasonable and God real.

GLENN FRANK.

CONTENTS

[ix]

CONTENTS

[x]

I. THE REASONABLENESS OF FAITH

Some faith demanded by fact of living; atheism solves nothing; the world without religion; religion as the laws of living; science and religion.

I. THE REASONABLENESS OF FAITH

IF the outstanding characteristic of the present age
had to be summed up in one word, undoubtedly
that word would be "scientific." Undoubtedly,
too, one of the by-products of the popularization
of science is the impression on the part of many
people that science is reasonable and can be completely proved, whereas religion is unreasonable
and cannot be proved. Religion and science are
thus contrasted in their minds, and feeling the
urge of the time to be scientific, such folk are
impelled to be irreligious. They adopt what they
consider a scientific attitude, and profess to believe
nothing that cannot be proved.

As a matter of fact, however, this attitude of
demanding absolute proof for everything is really
unscientific. It is unreasonable and untenable.
More than that, it is actually unlivable. And the
very people who make a profession of accepting
only what can be proved up to the hilt, do not live
by any such rule. One who tried to live con-

[3]

sistently by such a rule would land in an insane asylum.

For the very fact of living implies some faith, a belief in some things that one has not proved, and cannot prove. It is merely natural faith, it is true, but it is a genuine faith in the sense of being a belief in what cannot be demonstrated. Faith of this sort and life are so inextricably entangled that no one can escape faith except by escaping from life—or from reason. We do, in a very real sense, live by faith. The only people who manage to live without faith are the insane. Other people who profess to live entirely by reason, to believe nothing that they cannot prove by their reason, are making this profession only because they have not analyzed the situation far enough.

For instance, such people would be insulted if one questioned their parentage. But from the nature of the case, they cannot *know* who were their parents. They are taking on faith statements of others which they really cannot verify by their own investigation.

Faith is necessary, then, for any sort of family life. Without some faith between husband and wife, between parents and children, family existence would be unbearable. And the family is the basis of all society. If there were no faith in the home, and consequently no families, there could be no society.

All other human association, besides the family, is based on faith, on confidence in what really cannot be proved by the strictest reasoning. One must have faith in the integrity of the motorman who runs the subway, the engineer who drives the locomotive, the chauffeur of the taxi, the milkman and the baker, and the banker who holds one's money on deposit.

All of modern industry is built on credit of one sort or another. And credit is a phase of faith. Destroy that faith, and there would be a panic. In fact, a panic is merely a loss of commercial faith. The hardest boiled banker in Wall Street has to have faith in order to do business.

A scientist could not get started on an experiment if he did not have faith in some things, but insisted on proving up everything each day. How can he be sure, except by faith, that someone has not tampered with his scales, or adulterated his reagents? There are people of this suspicious disposition, but we all know of what it is a symptom, and where it leads if unchecked. I knew of one

[5]

man in an officers' training camp during the war who used to bring a sponge soaked in a germicidal solution to his meals and carefully wipe the table and his utensils. Poor fellow, if a German bullet or some germ did not get him, I suppose he is behind bars now. He needed more faith.

Professor E. C. Hayes, at the time of his death head of the department of sociology at the University of Illinois, and formerly president of the American Sociological Society, says that "no absolute division can be made between creeds and sciences. It is a difference of degree. . . . An Australian black fellow on a journey, finding that night is approaching while he is still far from his destination, takes a stone or clod and puts it up as high as he can reach in the fork of a tree to trig the sun. It is not a religious act, it is simply a piece of applied science" (*Introduction to the Study of Sociology*, p. 362, Appleton 6th edition).

Even more explicit is the statement of the late Professor Lester F. Ward, of Brown: "We cannot too strongly emphasize the paradox that pure science really rests on faith" (*Pure Sociology*, p. 6, N. Y., 1914). William James long ago pointed out that the principle of causality—without which there could be no science—"is as much an altar to an unknown God as the one that St. Paul found at Athens. All our scientific and philosophic ideals are altars to unknown Gods" ("The Dilemma of Determinism," in *The Will to Believe*, p. 147, N. Y., 1921). And Professor Franklin H. Giddings of Columbia does "not admit that science can get on without speculation. It cannot, as a distinguished scientific thinker said the other day, even get on without guessing" (*Principles of Sociology*, Preface, N. Y., 1896).

But probably the most damaging witness against science in opposition to faith is Professor A. N. Whitehead. The first of his Lowell Lectures at Harvard in 1925 was on the origins of modern science. Speaking of the scientific revolt against medieval philosophy, he said that "it is a great mistake to conceive of this historical revolt as an appeal to reason. On the contrary, it was through and through an anti-intellectualist movement. . . . And it was based on a recoil from the inflexible rationality of medieval thought" (*Science and the Modern World*, N. Y., Macmillan, 1926, p. 12). "Science has never shaken off the impress of its origin in the historical revolt of the later

Renaissance. It has remained predominantly an anti-rationalistic movement, based upon a naïve faith" (*idem*, p. 22).

This opinion of Whitehead will be so surprising to many persons that they will feel inclined to throw it out of court immediately. But a few isolated quotations cannot do justice to his position, and a reading of the whole lecture is to be recommended. Incidentally, it is worth noting that Whitehead holds that "the faith in the possibility of science, generated antecedently to the development of modern scientific theory, is an unconscious derivation from medieval theology" (*idem*, p. 18).

But it is not only all science that is ultimately based on faith. If one analyzes the situation carefully enough, one finds that all human achievement is the result of faith. Achievement is based on a confidence that something which has not really been proved by reason can nevertheless be accomplished. There would never have been airplanes if the Wright brothers had not had faith in the possibility of such machines. Lindbergh had "the spirit of St. Louis" in a deeper sense than he perhaps realized—in the sense of having a faith akin to the Crusader's—when he attempted

[8]

his epic flight to Paris. Now we have knowledge, because these possibilities have been demonstrated, but these pioneer men had only faith.

There would be no United States today if Washington had not had faith in the possibility of achieving freedom. He did not have knowledge, and from the nature of the case could not have had knowledge. He had faith in something that his reason could not prove, that could be proved only by the trial. To make that trial, with the gallows or the firing squad as reward for failure, required a far-reaching faith.

These arguments, however, are not meant to minimize the rôle of reason. My idea is merely to show the unreasonableness of that exaggerated attitude, assumed by some people, of never accepting anything that cannot be proved. They must see that they have to accept some things on faith —human faith—if they are to live at all. Life without faith, indeed, would be so intolerable that one might as well end it at once.

From this essential fact of human experience— that life predicates faith—the conclusion is legitimate that any view of life denying all faith is really unnatural. Such a view of life does not fit the facts, and so it is unreasonable. To put the matter in a somewhat paradoxical form, it is reasonable to have faith, and it is unreasonable to depend exclusively on reason.

Hence the man who attempts to face the universe and life without faith—at least human faith —is not scientific. For good science must fit in with life, it must work. If an engineer builds a bridge according to a particular formula for calculating stresses, and the bridge breaks down in spite of good material and workmanship, he knows that the formula was wrong. In the same way, if the formula requiring absolute proof for everything breaks under the strain of actual living, we know that the formula is wrong.

The man who professes to live without faith is unscientific, because he is not seeing life, and seeing it whole. And on the other hand, the man who realizes the need of faith in life is being really scientific. Now it is true that all this has to do with merely human faith. But this line of argument may fittingly be taken as the first step towards showing the reasonableness of religious faith. The attitude of the agnostic towards religious faith is often based on the assumption that he is a superior being who admits nothing he cannot prove. Therefore, to convince him that he is constantly admitting in other spheres what he cannot prove, will help to undermine his prejudice against religious faith.

II

There are some people who drift away from religious faith because of intellectual difficulties, and I admit quite frankly that there are difficulties connected with faith in God. But there are also difficulties on the other side. And the atheist or agnostic is not really liberal-minded if he does not consider those difficulties. Apart from any question of the truth or falsity of theism, I think I am safe in saying that atheism and agnosticism are intellectually unsatisfying. By this I mean that they solve nothing. The existence of sin and suffering are certainly grave difficulties for the believer. But sin and suffering are not eliminated by atheism or agnosticism, nor is the problem of their existence solved. One cannot rid the world of sin and suffering by ridding human beings of a belief in God.

The atheist suffers from cancer just as much as the theist; he undergoes the anguish of heart that comes from the loss of loved ones; he is injured just as deeply by the injustice of rascals. Sin and suffering remain for the atheist, despite his brave denial of any intelligent Being back of the universe. Denying an intelligent Creator does not make the universe any more intelligible, and it does not make the suffering and injustice any easier to bear.

I have said that the unbeliever suffers as much as the believer from the sins of others and from the weakness of his own body. But that is understating the case. In many instances he suffers more.

For even bodily suffering is largely psychological, and the unbeliever has not as soothing a psychological attitude as the believer. The mind has some influence over the body, and the believer's attitude of mind has a tendency to minimize physical suffering. He can look upon suffering as deserved by his sins, as a form of expiation for what he has done; or he can be sure, although he sees no explanation, that this is due to the limitations of his intellect, that there *is* a meaning in it all, and that some day he will understand.

And when we consider what may be called spiritual suffering—as, for instance, grief at the loss of loved ones—the influence of the mind is still more important. When an atheist stands beside the open grave of a wife, or child, or mother, who was dearer to him than his own life, he is face to face with an ultimate blank. *That* is the end for him. There is no faith in a future life, no belief in a possible reunion hereafter. For him the whole situation is just the product of blind mechanical forces, with no love, no intelligence, operating through them in any way. And yet, by some cruel joke, love and intelligence have been introduced into this atheist. The Ford car does not suffer when the mechanism of the universe dumps it upon a scrap heap, because it cannot know what is happening. But this atheist does know, and he suffers because he knows without understanding.

Now contrast this helpless, hopeless condition of the atheist with the serenity of the believer. The believer has his sorrow tempered by the conviction that an all-good God did have some purpose in this death. He may not be able to see the purpose, he may feel the loss keenly. But, nevertheless, he believes that some day he will see the meaning. His intellect is partly satisfied by this faith. And he has hope, too, that in a future life, where there is no sin and no suffering, he will once more be united with his loved one. His sense of loss cannot be as great as the atheist's, because it is only a temporary loss. It is the difference between time and eternity.

Of course, the mere fact that the believer suffers less in this life than the unbeliever, does not prove the believer right. But it does prove this—that unbelief does not solve the problems posited by life. Sin and suffering remain. And if belief can reduce suffering, it has at least to that extent solved the problem, just as the anesthetic of the doctor has temporarily conquered suffering. Moreover, the fact that a believer suffers less than an unbeliever proves that the believer gets more out of this life—irrespective of the next—than the unbeliever gets.

Some unbelievers realize that believers are profiting even in this life, and they have a wistful longing for faith. In an early number of *Plain Talk* (October, 1927) Mella Russell McCallum, who calls herself "an atheist, certainly an agnostic," expresses this attitude quite frankly. The God of Abraham, Isaac, and Jacob, seems to her entirely mythological, nor can she believe in the Trinity. "It just won't go down," she says. But she is keen enough in her self-analysis to continue:

[14]

"I wish it would go down, for to be sure in faith is a wonderful thing. I know, because I once had it. When one is sure, one can let the rest of the world go hang. But as things stand with me now, it is I who go hang. Not having any God on whom to cast my burdens, I must struggle with them alone, must myself be God. And I feel very inadequate at the task."

This unbeliever sees clearly that from a practical, pragmatic standpoint, there is more happiness in this world for the believer than for the unbeliever. To the query of her unbelieving friends, "But wouldn't you rather see things straight than be ignorantly happy?" she replied: "That's a beautiful theory, but my answer is 'No.' What difference does it make whether I see things straight or not? As a matter of fact, I'm all mixed up."

Considering "the question of mental peace," Miss McCallum asks: "Which class of people more nearly attains that goal?". And she replies: "The believers, of course. It is we [unbelievers] who are unhappy. We are so dreadfully stirred up about religion and man's relation to the universe. Such matters are settled for the believers. We [unbelievers] fuss and philosophize and apply

[15]

THE REASONABLENESS OF FAITH

science and history, and get worried, while the
believers, having things managed automatically
through faith, go calmly onward. And as they
go, they often achieve a dignity, a simplicity, and
so a pattern of life, that is very beautiful."

It has sometimes been said by unbelievers that
faith in another world has been used as a sort of
anodyne to dull the common herd of men to the
sufferings of this life, in order that they should
not rebel against the upper classes who are getting
so much more of this world's goods. In this way,
so it is claimed, religious faith has militated
against a betterment of conditions here and now.
And the unbelievers sometimes go on to assert that
all improvement is posited upon doubt, that all the
advances of humanity have been due to the rebels
against religion.

But besides pointing out that, as a matter of
fact, believers achieve more happiness here on
earth than unbelievers, Miss McCallum also
realizes that it is the believers who are laboring to
relieve human suffering, who are gradually making life better here on earth. She points to "such
things as undernourished children, and exploited
stupidity, and disease that thrives through ignorance." "Are the atheists, as a body," she asks,

[16]

"doing anything about such matters? Are there any fresh air camps backed by atheist organizations, or any great hospitals, with plenty of free beds, or groups to give a hungry man a bowl of soup and put him to bed?"

This is something on which everyone can check up. There are innumerable religious and nonsectarian charitable organizations in this country doing admirable charitable work. But I do not know of a single organization of atheists in the field. Does the Society for the Advancement of Atheism conduct a hospital for the cancerous poor? or for lepers, where unbelieving Damians are consecrating their lives with the certainty of ultimately themselves contracting this loathsome disease? If atheistic organizations are thus serving humanity, they are certainly succeeding in hiding their light under a bushel.

And while belief in a future life may help to dull the sufferings of this existence, and so check a spirit of rebelliousness, there is another angle to the situation. Men with plenty of this world's goods, who believe that this life is worthless compared with eternal life hereafter, and who also believe that they are going to be happier hereafter by helping less fortunate people here and now, are much more likely to share their temporal prosperity with others than are men who think that this is all they are ever going to have.

Of course, there are many individual unbelievers who put some individual believers to shame by the nobility of their lives. But as a body, atheists are not doing the things to improve life that believers are doing as a body. And probably the nobility of individual atheists is due in part to a certain absorption from a religious environment. For we do not have unbelievers in a completely unbelieving world. All religion cannot be excluded so as to get unbelief as it would be in itself.

But in imagination we can suppose that all belief had disappeared. There would be no Sisters of Charity to nurse the sick, no Little Sisters of the Poor to look after the aged, no Salvation Army, no stimulating belief in anything greater than one's self, no restraining influence from belief in an avenging God. Would life be worth living, as Mallock asked? What kind of world would this be?

At least one atheist or agnostic, Miss McCallum, has a frank answer: "I'm inclined to think," she says, "it would be a hell of a world."

III

Certain considerations have been pointed out to show the necessity of some faith—of belief in what we have not proved—and consequently the unscientific character of wholesale unbelief. Nevertheless one of the strongest influences making against religious faith is the impression that there is an insoluble conflict between science and faith. And many persons conclude, as a corollary, that, therefore, atheists and agnostics are scientific, and religious folk are unscientific. Consequently, as science dominates the modern world, and no one would think of giving up science, the alternative is to give up religious faith.

Now the first point I want to make in trying to remove such an impression, is the fact that many great scientists have seen no such conflict between science and religion. This religio-scientific conflict has been developed largely by third-rate popularizers of science, rather than by the great original thinkers in scientific fields.

If we go back, for example, to a man such as Pasteur, who stands out as a supreme leader of science, the founder of modern biology, one of the greatest benefactors that the world has known, one whose methods are still in use and universally familiar—if we go back to such a man, we find that he was deeply religious. He himself tells us that he had the faith of a Breton peasant, and that he hoped some day he might have the faith of a Breton peasant's wife. Pasteur saw no conflict between his Catholic religion and his scientific outlook on life.

Coming closer to our own day, I suppose that everyone will agree that Lord Kelvin was one of the greatest scientists of the nineteenth and early twentieth century. Like Pasteur, Lord Kelvin had a religious attitude towards the universe. His scientific studies did not undermine his religious faith. In May, 1903, at University College, London, Lord Kelvin said: "Science positively affirms creative power. . . . We are absolutely forced by science to admit and to believe with absolute confidence in a Directive Power. . . . If you think strongly enough you will be forced by science to the belief in God, which is the foundation of all Religion. You will find science not antagonistic, but helpful to Religion" (*The Life of William Thomson*, by S. P. Thompson, II, pp. 1098-1099, N. Y., Macmillan, 1910).

Since Lord Kelvin pronounced this emphatic

declaration of faith, the great scientists have become more rather than less religious. Some professors like Leuba or Elmer Barnes, who are themselves not scientists, may still have an 1875 model of the relations between science and religion, but men like Millikan take a different view. Professor Millikan has been president of the American Physical Society, and in 1923 received the Nobel prize for isolating and measuring the ultimate electrical unit, the electron. He is no mere popularizer of the work of others, but is an original investigator, an outstanding figure in scientific circles.

"We should use the word 'God,'" says Millikan, "to describe what is behind the mystery of existence. . . . I have never known a thinking man who did not believe in God . . . Everyone who reflects at all believes, in one way or another, in God. . . . To me it is unthinkable that a real atheist should exist at all. . . . It seems to me as obvious as breathing that every man who is sufficiently in his senses to recognize his own inability to comprehend the problem of existence, to understand whence he came and whither he is going, must in the very admission of that ignorance and finiteness recognize the existence of a something, a Power, and Being in whom and because of whom he himself 'lives and moves and has his being.' That power, that something, that existence, we call God" (*World's Work*, April, 1926, pp. 665, 666).

Professor Pupin, of Columbia University, has told us quite frankly that his scientific studies have made him a more devout Christian. And Professor Pupin stands in the very front rank of modern scientists. He, too, has not only a national, but an international reputation. He, too, is no mere popularizer of science, but is himself an original investigator.

"The realities of both physical science and organic science," Pupin tells us, "reveal a God, a divine intelligence that we, as intelligent beings can depend upon. . . . Science leads us straight to a belief in God, and this is the foundation of religion. . . . Science does not prevent a man from being a Christian, but makes him a better Christian. It has made me a better Christian." (Quoted in *The Literary Digest*, October 1, 1927, p. 33).

The first point I want to make, then, is that many great leaders of science saw and see absolutely no conflict between science and religion.

Remember, too, in the second place, that the

attitude which assumes a necessary conflict between science and religion, assumes, too, that in this conflict science is always right and religion always wrong. Now that attitude is entirely unjustified by the facts.

Naïvely identifying science with the latest scientific teaching, popularizers contrast what science has to tell us today with what some medieval theologians had to say, perhaps on a question such as the motion of the earth around the sun. And because the ancient theologians have been discredited in their opposition to the Copernican system, the upholders of a necessary conflict between science and religion jump to the conclusion that religion has been discredited in everything.

But we should remember that the scientists of the days of Galileo, or of Julius Cæsar, have been as much discredited as the theologians of those times. Science is not a complete and unchangeable statement of truth that is in the end always triumphant. Science changes from age to age, from generation to generation. Twenty-five years ago, when I was in college, the teaching of science in regard to the ultimate constitution of matter was quite different from the present scientific teaching. At one time or another "science" has taught that the earth was the center of the universe, that the blood did not circulate, that tuberculosis was hereditary, that acquired characteristics are transmitted, and numerous other propositions that are now denied by "science." At the beginning of the nineteenth century "science," in order to cure certain diseases took away part of a man's blood by what was called bleeding; at the beginning of the twentieth century, "science" to cure the same diseases, gives a man more blood by transfusion.

Naturally, theologians have sometimes allowed their "scientific" knowledge to influence their theology, and they have taken for granted that revelation was to be interpreted in accordance with the traditional "science" they learned in their own school days. Then when some progressive scientists proposed a new theory, the theologians—in union with most of the scientists of that time—opposed the new theory. The conflict, however, was not really between true science and definitive religion, but rather between scientists and theologians. Nor was that conflict any more bitter and obscurantist than the disputes between one group of scientists and another.

In a very interesting book called *Science and*

THE REASONABLENESS OF FAITH

Scientists in the Nineteenth Century (London, Sheldon Press, 1925), Dr. R. H. Murray tells the story of the opposition to each new scientific theory—an opposition, be it carefully noted, not from theologians in the name of religion, but from scientists in the name of science. The famous Dr. Osler once said that the human mind tends to fossilize after the age of forty or forty-five; and consequently it is very difficult for men who have passed that age to receive new ideas. Therefore men educated in their university youth in a particular scientific attitude find it hard to adjust themselves to changes in their special field of learning. The conflict is usually between these older men and younger ones. It is a defect of human nature and has nothing whatever to do with any essential conflict between science and religion.

In the preface to his book, Dr. Murray has a very apposite passage which I wish to quote. "If one reads," he says, "such a tenth-rate book as J. W. Draper's *History of the Conflict between Religion and Science,* or even such a book as A. D. White's *History of the Warfare of Science with Theology,* one is conscious that both authors assume unquestioningly that the theologian is moved by prepossessions, whereas the man of science is moved by nothing else than the desire to ascertain the facts as they actually are. Would that it were so with all men of science! [But] it might have occurred to these authors that the history of science bears no testimony to the accuracy of their assumption, and indeed one main purpose in writing this book has been to prove that there are just as many preconceived notions in science as there are in theology. . . . I have enough faith in the candor of men of science," continues Dr. Murray, "to think that if—it is a big If—it is possible to convince them that there are every whit as many prepossessions in their departments as there are in theology, we shall hear less of the warfare between science and theology. For a similar warfare is characteristic of *every* department of human knowledge" (p. vIII).

In reality, the conflict is not so much between science and religion, or even between scientists and churchmen, as it is between a few advanced scientists and the natural inertia of the human mind. The popularizers of science, who imagine a necessary conflict between science and religion, should remember the words of Professor Lynn Thorndike, of Columbia, in his *History of Magic:* "One

[26]

can well imagine that a future age may regard much of the learning even of our time as almost as futile, superstitious, fantastic in method, and irrelevant to the ends sought, as were primitive man's methods of producing rain, Egyptian amulets to cure disease, or medieval blood-letting according to the phases of the moon" (Vol. II, p. 979, N. Y., Macmillan, 1923).

Inasmuch as religion to us is revealed truth, and science is truth gained by the observation of physical phenomena, there can be no real conflict between science and religion. If there seems to be a conflict, it is because either the theologian or the scientist has gone beyond his legitimate sphere— and I think the fair-minded historian will admit that the fault has been more often on the side of the scientists.

Cardinal Newman, in a lecture on "Christianity and Scientific Investigation," has put our position with extraordinary force and clearness. "He who believes in Revelation," says the Cardinal, "with that absolute faith which is the prerogative of a Catholic, is not the nervous creature who startles at every sudden sound. . . . He laughs at the idea that anything can be discovered by any other scientific method, which can contradict any one

[27]

of the dogmas of his religion. . . . He is sure
. . . that, if anything seems to be proved by
astronomer, or geologist, or chronologist, or anti-
quarian, or ethnologist, in contradiction to the
dogmas of faith, that point will eventually turn
out, first, *not* to be proved, or secondly, not *contradictory*, or thirdly, not contradictory to anything *really revealed*, but to something that has
been confused with revelation" (*The Idea of a
University*, p. 466, N. Y., Longmans).

IV

There is, then, no essential conflict between
science and religion. On the contrary, the more
science approximates to truth, the more support it
gives to the fundamental tenets of religious faith.
And sometimes a practical scientific advance, like
radio, tends to support one or other religious belief. Very briefly, then, I shall try to show how
broadcasting throws some light upon the idea of
a divine revelation.

What happens in broadcasting is essentially that
there are sent out waves of some sort of force
which travel enormous distances, and which can be
picked up by proper instruments and turned back
into something like the original human voice. It

is not the voice that travels, as is the case, we may say, when a man shouts, and is heard at a distance. Then the sound fills every intervening space, and anyone with ears can hear the words. But in broadcasting by radio, the air is perfectly quiet as far as unassisted ears are concerned, though it is filled with potential messages. Certain instruments are needed in order to hear. Only the fortunate ones with properly sensitive sets can listen in.

Now it is apparent that this bears some analogy to the idea of divine revelation. We believe that back of this universe as its Creator is a personal Being Who is thought and love, because He is the supreme expression of intellect and will. We see in Him our feeble faculties of knowing and loving raised to infinity. The constant activity of this Person is sending its waves of force, as it were, throughout the whole universe. Everyone's room is filled with His messages, but the messages need to be turned into human language by the properly sensitive recipients.

In most cases, men do not hear God's words because they are busy about other things. They are tuning in their receiving sets on the things of time—on making money, and enjoying the flesh

[29]

pots of Egypt. . Their dials are fixed so as to receive sensual rather than spiritual messages. They are like Martha, busy about many things—in a great many cases excellent things, but which keep them from giving themselves, like Mary, to the one thing necessary, and getting the message Mary received.

But now and then in the long history of the human race, there have been individuals who supremely wanted something beside the things of time and the body. They were interested in the soul. And by constant meditation, by continual experimentation, we may say, they finally got what we may with all reverence call God's broadcasting station. With some faculty other than the bodily ear, they heard His whisperings coming to them across the abyss of time, and for the benefit of their fellow men, they wrote down what they had heard. These hearers or seers were what we call inspired, and the books they wrote constitute our Bible.

Does not the very modern scientific phenomenon of radio broadcasting and reception make it easier to believe that some such communication is possible between God and man? And if we accept the theory of some scientists that each human brain is a miniature broadcasting station, sending out its waves upon the air every time it thinks, the analogy is even closer. For if human thinking so affects the air, why should not God's thinking do so, too?

And this idea of each brain being a broadcasting station bears upon another point of our religious belief: the possibility of prayer, and of communication in some way with those who have died. Except in the somewhat rare cases of telepathic powers, we cannot pick up the messages of these tiny brain stations. But may we not believe that when the human soul is freed from its imprisonment in the body, it may be sufficiently sensitive to hear and understand what we who are still on earth are thinking and praying?

Under our present limitations we can listen to only one station at a time. If we get WEAF, we cannot at the same moment have WLWL. But may not that be a limitation imposed upon us by out material bodies? In a future existence, where there will be no clayey bodies such as we have now, may it not be possible to have faculties that can listen attentively to all one's friends and relatives back on earth at the same time, if they happen to be turning their thoughts to us?

[31]

Of course, this is only an analogy. I do not offer it as a proof that God has made a revelation, or that the saints in heaven can hear our prayers. But it does seem to me to make it somewhat easier to believe in a revelation, and in what the Apostles' Creed calls the Communion of Saints. Like every comparison, however, it limps somewhat, and no doubt many of you can see the limping.

In regard to an even more fundamental religious belief, the existence of a personal God, it seems to me that science offers the believer some help. The idea of evolution is dominant today in scientific circles. And while to some theologians the word is anathema, there have been great saints, such as St. Augustine and Thomas Aquinas, who thought that this idea gave us a better concept of God's creative power than the belief in immediate interference for each species.

More than thirty years ago, when it must be admitted some theologians had not become orientated to the theory of evolution, Father J. A. Zahm wrote: "To say that Evolution is agnostic or atheistic in tendency, if not in fact, is to betray a lamentable ignorance of what it actually teaches. . . . Rather should it be affirmed that Evolution, in so far as it is true, makes for religion: because it needs must be that a true theory of the origin and development of things must, when properly understood and applied, both strengthen and illustrate the teachings of faith" (*Evolution and Dogma*, p. 389, Chicago, McBride, 1896).

Father Zahm then goes on to quote Professor Fiske as saying: "When from the dawn of life, we see all things working together towards the Evolution of the highest spiritual attributes or man, we know, however the words may stumble in which we try to say it, that God is in the deepest sense a moral being" (*The Idea of God*, p. 167). "The doctrine of Evolution destroys the conception of the world as a machine. It makes God our constant refuge and support, and nature His true revelation. Though science must destroy mythology, it can never destroy religion; and to the astronomer of the future, as well as to the Psalmist of old, 'the heavens will declare the glory of God'" (*Outlines of Cosmic Philosophy*, Vol. II, p. 416).

And when to the idea of evolution, science adds the modern theory of matter, then belief in creation by a spiritual Person becomes easier still. For modern science has reduced matter to little more than points of force. Bertrand Russell, the English mathematician, in a recent book (*Philosophy*, 6, N. Y., 1927, Norton) speaks of matter as "waves progressing outward from a center." And with this de-materializing of matter, if I may use that word, the relation between a purely spiritual Being and this material universe becomes more understandable. Incidentally, it is interesting to note that Boscovitch, an eighteenth century Jesuit philosopher, seems to have arrived at about the same concept of matter before it was possible to prove it by any laboratory experiments.

As this modern theory of matter throws some light upon the beginning of things, so it throws some light upon the end of us all, or rather upon the possibility of some sort of spiritualized body actually rising from the dead for each of us. The more matter is de-materialized by science, the more plausible becomes the clothing of spirits with material bodies in the next life. And the old scientific or supposedly scientific conundrum of what would happen to particles of matter that had formed parts of several human bodies, since there would be innumerable claimants to the same particles of matter on judgment day, becomes fantastic.

But I do not wish to make the mistake of tying

up religion and science. That mistake has been made in the past with consequences lasting to our own time. For when science changed, then religion suffered. And sometimes the theologians, wedded to one concept of science, were averse to giving up that concept. They called upon their theology to support their science, and identified religion with something extrinsic and accidental.

The science of today will not be the science of tomorrow. The next generation may blithely scrap the theory of evolution and the electronic constitution of matter. When that scrapping process comes, if it does come, our religious faith should not be affected by having been made dependent upon a passing attitude of science. But the religion of today, in so far as it is a correct understanding of God's revelation, must endure forever.

Moreover, I am not a scientist. In the few ideas I have thrown out, I am merely a sort of popularizer of science. I have taken my understanding of the scientific theories advanced by other people, and have applied them to religion. If I have made a mistake in my understanding of science, that does not really affect the religion I have expounded. Religion depends no more upon the Copernican system than upon the Ptolemaic, upon the evolution than upon fixity of species, upon protons and electrons than upon atoms and molecules. Scientific theories may come and go, but religion remains eternally true.

"There is no God like the God of the righteous . . . His dwelling is above, and underneath are the everlasting arms" (Deuteronomy 33: 26, 27).

v

Before leaving the question of religious faith in general, there is another mistaken attitude which it would be well to consider. It is that religion is essentially unnatural and gloomy, fettering the believer with bonds that take all the joy out of life. And by implication, the unbeliever is imagined as a carefree, happy individual who is not bound by any foolish superstitions about right and wrong. Kipling has well expressed this attitude in his poem "On the Road to Mandalay." The songster desires to be shipped somewhere East of Suez, "where there aren't no Ten Commandments and the best is like the worst."

To grasp the right view of religion is to realize that it is a set of rules to enable us to get more out of the game of life. The Ten Commandments sum up the wisdom of God and of man as to how we have to act if we are to win. At times they may seem to cramp our style somewhat, but in the long run the man who keeps these Commandments gets more out of living than the man who breaks them.

Everyone who undertakes to play bridge probably feels at first that certain rules formulated by the experts are more of a hindrance than a help. But every experienced player knows that the man who disregards all such rules will be easy pickings. And the same thing is true in all our sports. There is an art about holding a tennis racket or a golf club that does not come naturally with the first attempt. We need to learn the rules that wide experience has taught others as to the best way of doing things.

If this be true of such a relatively simple thing as bridge, or golf, or tennis, it is very much truer of the complicated game of life. The man who says he will not be hampered by rules, that he will trust to his instincts, that he will seize the pleasure of the moment—take as many tricks as possible immediately, as it were—is bound to get set, to use a bridge term. In the long run his score will not be as high as that of the more careful player who follows certain rules.

Perhaps Christ had something of this in mind when He said that He came that we might have life, and have it more abundantly. Religious life implies rich living. It means getting more out of time, to say nothing of eternity. We are not all dealt the same hands by any means, but if we follow the rules we can get more out of what we have than by going it blindly and trusting merely to luck. And so we ought to get away from the conception of religion that it is something negative, holding us in; and we ought to think of it as a positive help to take two tricks where otherwise we might make only one.

It may have been with some thought of leading us away from a negative attitude towards religion that Christ summed up the whole Law and the Prophets in two positive commandments of love. Under the Old Dispensation we had a decalogue of don'ts. Thou shalt not do this, and that, and that. But Christ got away from negative don'ts to positive do's. Thou shalt love God with thy whole heart, He said, and thy neighbor as thyself. Do this and thou shalt have eternal life.

But not only eternal life. For Christ promised an earthly reward—possession of the land—for practising one of the beatitudes. And it is significant that Christ adopted a pragmatic attitude toward religion. The religion of any particular individual, according to Christ, was to be judged by results. A good tree, He told us, must bring forth good fruit. We do not have to wait until some vague future time or some eternity to judge of religion. We can tell its fruits here in this world; and one of its fruits is enrichment of living. Religion should be ordering our lives in such a way that we are really solving life's problems better than we could solve them without religion, that we are therefore making our lives richer and nobler because of religion.

It is true that this temporal result of religion cannot be demonstrated like a proposition in geometry. There will always be room to doubt Christ's insight into the workings of life. We have faith, not knowledge. We are not, as it were, betting upon an absolutely sure thing. The possibility remains of gambling magnificently, of staking our religious faith in Christ's wisdom against the superficial appearances of life.

For we must admit that sometimes a man may

seem to gain from the standpoint of this life by violating one of the Ten Commandments, or the Commandment to love his neighbor as himself. But there are several considerations we should bear in mind in judging any such appearances.

One consideration is that the gain may be only temporary, even in this life; as an amateur bridge player may by luck have a run of success though going counter to the expert's rules, yet the long pull will decide against him. An old proverb says, call no man happy till his death. In the end, a man loses by breaking the rules of the game of life as summed up in the Commandments. Many a suicide's death demonstrates how blank and empty life was to a seemingly successful man, because he did not have the enriching influences of religious faith.

And another consideration is that usually we see only the superficial aspects of a man's life. Now and then, however, in some way publicity overtakes an individual, and we realize that the man we thought had gained so much by shady practices has in reality been losing all along. Even the worldly-minded have coined the phrase, "honesty is the best policy." It is an acknowledgment that to be honest is not only a divine commandment of religion, but also a dictate of worldly prudence. Men who see life straight realize that taken by and large there is no way of beating the game. The rewards come to the man who follows the rules.

Moreover, in judging anyone's life, we should be careful to make certain that the fruits come really from his religion. It is possible for a man to read a manual on bridge, and to profess to follow it, when in reality he has violated some of its most fundamental rules. And similarly, it is possible for a man to make a profession of religion, and yet to divorce his conduct from the implications of that faith.

St. James noticed this phenomenon centuries ago, and he warned his readers to be doers of the word and not hearers only. He applied to religious profession the same test of results that Christ had formulated, and that I am now advocating. "What shall it profit," he asks, "if a man say he hath faith, but hath not works? Shall faith be able to save him? And if a brother or sister be naked, and want daily food: and one of you say to them: Go in peace, be ye warmed and filled; yet give them not those things that are necessary for the body, what shall it profit? So

faith also, if it have not works, is dead in itself"
(I: 22, II: 14-17).

Hence, in speaking of religious faith, I have
meant a genuine faith that is necessarily translated
into works. It is not enough to profess with the
lips a love for one's neighbor. That profession
is empty and futile unless it is accompanied by
deeds. Consequently, in judging religious faith,
we must be careful to note if the conduct of individuals is a result of their profession, or a result
of failure to live up to that profession. The fact
that a man professes religion, and then acts contrary to his profession, is not a condemnation of
religion, but a condemnation of the man.

We often hear the complaint that many people
professing Christianity were not interested in seeing less fortunate men get a square deal, that they
really did not love their neighbors as themselves.
And we must admit that this complaint is often
justified. Many professed Christians are not living up to the principles of Christ's religion. But
their conduct is not justly attributable to their
religious profession, to Christianity. On the contrary, it is a direct contradiction of Christianity.
It proves the falseness of their profession, and not

the falseness of the Christian religion. Nothing in the rules of Christianity leads them to act in this way.

Similar differences between faith and practice are all around us. I have known hospitals where there were common drinking cups. But that did not lead me to discard the germ theory. It only made me wonder at the inconsistency of the people who were running the hospital.

And so if we find that the conduct of some people does not square with their religious profession, we should not therefore give up religion. If a man gets a counterfeit twenty dollar bill, he does not conclude that all money is bad, and throw away the rest of the money he has. Neither should the existence of counterfeit religion, or of hypocritical professors of religion, lead us to condemn all religion. Counterfeiters of religion really prove the worth of genuine religion, for no one counterfeits what is worthless.

And so I close these talks on faith with the reiteration that faith is the most important thing in life. Faith of some sort, if only faith in our own parentage, or in the skill of the subway motorman, is absolutely essential for life. And

[43]

religious faith is the only solution we have for the knottiest problems confronting us—suffering and death. To men of faith it is given not only to conquer the citadels of heaven, but also to rule their lives on earth so as to get the most out of the endowments they have received.

II. THE DIFFICULTIES OF ATHEISM

Evolution implies universe existing for only a limited time; otherwise repetition; same is true of theory of relativity; also the diffusion of heat; design implies a Designer.

II. THE DIFFICULTIES OF ATHEISM

I

OF course, there are intellectual difficulties connected with the existence of God. But there are difficulties connected with a denial of His existence. And young people so frequently make the mistake of concentrating their attention on the difficulties of theism, and of ignoring the difficulties of atheism, that I want you to consider for a few minutes some of the difficulties inherent in the atheistic position.

We are living in an age when science dominates thinking, and there is at least an implied assumption that because science has explained so many things that were once attributed to direct divine intervention, it can explain everything without God. This is truer, perhaps, in regard to the theory of evolution than it is in regard to any other scientific teaching. And I must confess that the attitude of many theologians has been largely responsible for this idea. They fought the theory of evolution on theological grounds, called it infidel and atheistic, and a large part of the world took them at their word.

Nevertheless, out of deference to this prejudice on the part of some that the scientific doctrine of evolution has ruled out God, our consideration of God's existence may well begin by showing that so far from doing away with the intellectual necessity of postulating God as Creator, the scientific theory of evolution on the contrary rather strengthens this necessity.

There is only one alternative to creation, and that is eternal existence. Nothing can come of nothing. That is a fundamental principle underlying all science. If this universe is not eternal, then until its existence there was no matter. And what brought this universe into existence out of nothing? Because it is impossible to conceive of a material universe creating itself, bringing itself into existence out of nothingness, materialists have frankly accepted the alternative that this material universe actually has existed forever, for all eternity.

There have been philosophers who have seen no essential impossibility in an eternally existing universe. But the theory of evolution rather *tends* to show that this particular universe in which we live has not been eternal. I do not mean to say that evolution completely disproves the eternity of this universe, but only that it is evidence looking in the direction of a purely temporal world.

For evolution implies change. Inherent in the very idea of evolution is the idea of change. The process of changing, or of evolving, then, must either have been going on for all eternity, or it must have had a beginning.

Assuming for the moment, that this process of evolving had a beginning, what would be the consequences? If evolution had a beginning in an eternal universe, that means the universe was previously existing absolutely without change. We have really gotten back to the same intellectual problem involved in saying that the universe as a whole had a beginning. For if until evolution started there was absolutely no change in the universe, then how did this changing world come out of it? If it was the nature of the universe to exist unchangingly, what altered its nature, so that now it exists in a process of change? There is just as big a problem here as in self-creation. It would be intellectually necessary to postulate something outside the material universe that started the first change.

Consequently, either evolution has continued for all eternity, or it has been introduced into a changeless universe. But both horns of this dilemma are untenable. For there can be, on the materialistic assumption, nothing outside the universe to start a change. And on scientific principles, if at one time the universe was changeless, there would be nothing in the universe to cause a change.

If we assume some very rarefied substance such as ether, absolutely homogeneous, evolution could not get a start. It is useless to say that different stresses in different parts of this homogeneous substance set up a change. For then we have abandoned the hypothesis of an absolutely homogeneous substance. There was heterogeneity to start with, and the changes would have been eternal.

Anyone who postulates an absolutely homogeneous mass for the universe is in an intellectual blind alley. There is no way of getting away from that homogeneity into a universe of heterogeneity, except by introducing something from the outside. And then we have God. Not necessarily, by this argument, the personal God of the theist, but still a Being transcending the material world.

The other horn of the dilemma I suggested a minute ago, was that the universe should have been changing from all eternity. But that, too, is improbable on the theory of evolution. For if evolution had been proceeding from all eternity, it would have been completed by now. To be evolving implies something towards which the universe is evolving, as well as something away from which it is evolving. Eternal evolution connotes more than an infinite series of changes, inasmuch as it implies a progressive series; and a series of progressive states, in which each state is causally dependent upon the preceding.

Now, if the evolving universe has existed only a certain length of time—no matter how great that time is—then it can still be going on evolving towards its ultimate goal. But if it has been evolving absolutely forever, then it must have arrived at that goal. Otherwise, the word "eternity" is robbed of its meaning. You really limit "eternity," and in spite of the term you admit that evolution has been going on for only a limited period.

Scientists tell us that a certain number of million

years ago the universe was very different from what it is now. If we go back through this process of evolution, we find that at some time in the past there were no men, no animals, no living things at all in the universe. A certain number of million—of billion, or trillion—years has brought the universe to just the degree of evolution we know today.

But evolution must work both ways. If the world was different a few hundred million years ago, then if we go forward in imagination a few hundred million years, we would find a world different from what it is now. Niagara would have worn away more of its rocky bed, the ocean would be saltier, the destruction of forests would have affected climate, perhaps new species of animals would have been evolved, some suns would have burnt out. At any rate, evolution implies that the universe would have changed considerably in proportion to the length of time involved.

However, if eternity means anything, it means something more than any particular number of million years. Consequently, if the universe has existed absolutely for all eternity, then it has existed long enough to be farther along on the path of evolution. For it has existed longer than the millions of years necessary to produce the present phase of evolution. Otherwise, the word "eternity" is not being used in a strict sense of duration absolutely forever. Eternity becomes really a limited period of time, and a beginning is implied.

The evolutionary materialist who thinks that he has eliminated the need of God by affirming the eternity of the material universe gets himself into this awkward position. For if geologists and astronomers assign any certain number of million years as the time required to produce this particular condition of the universe, the materialist, to be consistent, must reply: "No, the universe has existed longer than that, since it has existed for all eternity."

It should be perfectly evident, however, that if the material universe has existed for more than the time necessary to produce the present conditions, then it ought to be farther advanced in evolution. That is equivalent to saying that this is not today, but a million years hence. We are not ourselves, but some future beings who will be evolved. And as all that is foolishness, would turn science topsy turvy, in fact would make all science impossible, the conclusion must be that the universe has not existed for all eternity, but only for a limited time. We cannot calculate that time accurately, it may be greater than any particular estimate of scientists, but nevertheless it is limited.

But once this is admitted, the eternal existence of the universe is denied. And if it has not existed forever, when did it begin to exist, and how did it come into existence? We are forced back upon the very same difficulty we discussed a little while ago. And so the theory of evolution, instead of invalidating the theist's position, really strengthens it. Evolution renders more graphic and understandable the idea that an eternal material universe is impossible.

II

The theory of evolution applied to a material changing universe that has existed for all eternity would lead to even more striking difficulties than the one just mentioned. For, as pointed out, evolution implies something towards which the universe is evolving. Now if the word eternity means anything more than an indefinitely long time, the universe would have arrived at that goal.

And having arrived at that goal, it would either have to stop, or else repeat the process of evolving from some primal nebula up through all the more

complicated structures to the final terminus of evolution. The process suggests the hands of a clock.
When they have passed through all the combinations possible from twelve to twelve, they go on
through the same combinations again. Or it would
be like a gold fish swimming in a bowl. Increase
the size of the bowl, and the time needed for going
around it is increased. But if the fish has time
enough he will get around. And if it takes a certain length of time to make the circuit once, then
if you increase to eternity the time the fish has,
you increase the number of times the fish can go
around the bowl. He will have gone around not
only once, but an indefinite number of times.
There will be a repetition of his experiences.

The essence of this point is not changed by making the bowl as big as our universe and increasing
the number of fish to correspond to all our heav-
enly bodies. It would increase the length of time
required to go through the whole process of evolution, but eternity would be more than enough for
this. If the universe has actually existed forever,
then the process of evolution has completed itself
any number of times, and there has been repetition.

Let me try to bring this home to you. Not only

once in the past, but innumerable times, the universe reached a point where earth and sea and sky were just as they are tonight; where men had achieved just the mechanical triumphs they have today in the way of autos and airplanes and radio; and just such a man as I stood before just such an audience in just such a room as this and spoke exactly the same words I am speaking.

That is the conclusion materialism leads to. If this is a purely material universe, dominated entirely by mechanistic laws so that nothing could ever happen otherwise, and ruled by a process of evolution that is inexorably working out along lines that are absolutely determined for it, and this process has been going on for all eternity, then there must have been repetition.

I suppose that a person can believe that. But certainly it is a large order. And, too, it certainly puts more strain upon one's credulity than anything Christianity demands of its followers. Creation, the Incarnation, the Resurrection are the tiniest gnats beside this gigantic camel which the materialists want us to swallow. Is it not easier to believe in God than to believe in this indefinite repetition?

Let me sum up the bearing of the theory of evolution on the existence of God. Evolution, I have said, implies either that the process of evolution has been going on for only a limited time; or else that the universe has been evolving long enough to be different from what it is now; indeed that there should have been a completion and a repetition of the process of evolution.

Since I find it too great a strain upon my faith and my intelligence to believe that the universe is different from what it is; or that it is simply at the same spot in the process of evolution that it has reached innumerable times in the past; I choose to believe that the universe has existed for only a limited time.

But if the universe has existed for only a limited time, how did it come into existence? Of course, it could not have brought itself into existence, for that would imply acting before existing. We are forced back upon the alternative that something outside the universe must have brought it into existence. And we call that something God.

It is true that this does not prove the God of the theists, endowed with free will and intelligence, all-good and all-loving, personally interested in each one of us. But one cannot prove everything at once. The rest will have to hold

[57]

over for another time. It is sufficient now to get clearly the idea that the scientific theory of evolution tends to disprove the eternal existence of the material universe. And, consequently, evolution tends to uphold a belief in God.

It would be well, however, to touch upon one other point. The thought may have suggested itself: If the material universe cannot have existed for all eternity, then how can God have existed for all eternity? Is there not the same difficulty for the theist as for the materialist? Do we not ultimately come to a blank non-existence?

No, because the same difficulties involved in the eternal existence of a material universe constantly changing or evolving are not implied in the eternal existence of a pure spirit that is unchangeable. It is possible to conceive of such a pure spirit. And while His relations with a changing, temporal universe offer difficulties for the theist, they are not by any means as serious as the difficulties connected with denying His existence.

III

We may frankly admit that there are some intellectual difficulties connected with theism. And this is why some persons can remain atheists and agnostics, and why some others who begin as theists finally lose their faith. They have concentrated too exclusively on the difficulties of theism, and they have failed to take sufficiently into consideration the difficulties that follow from eliminating God. Such people are suffering from a one-sided development. What they need is a broader view of the problems.

And so it is advisable to approach the question of God's existence largely from this negative side, by considering some of the intellectual difficulties inherent in trying to explain the material universe without God. And because the objections of atheists are frequently drawn from science, we began with a difficulty on their side that is tied in with the theory of evolution. Against the eternal existence of the material universe, you were previously asked to consider that the process of evolution would have been completed; and not only completed but, on such a supposition, repeated. For evolution implies something towards which the universe is evolving, and eternity would be long enough to have arrived there, and to have gone round again in a circle, as it were.

This objection was drawn from evolution. But the same idea of completion and repetition can also be derived from another angle of science.

Most of us know little about Einstein's theory of relativity. But one point in this theory has a bearing on the present discussion, and that is the finiteness of the material universe. Scholastic philosophers, considering the question from a metaphysical standpoint, long ago declared that the material universe had to be limited. And now this ultra-modern scientific theory confirms their view. Relativity seems to presuppose that the material universe cannot be infinite, that it must be limited.

Bertrand Russell in his book called *The A B C of Relativity* (Harper's, 1925), says: "Some very interesting speculations are connected with the theory of relativity. . . . One of the most fascinating is the suggestion that the universe may be of finite extent. Two somewhat different finite universes have been constructed, one by Einstein, the other by De Sitter (pp. 163, 164). "There are certain reasons," continues Russell, "for thinking that the total amount of matter in the universe is limited" (p. 164). And then to make perfectly clear the sense in which he is using the word

[60]

"finite," he adds: "We must therefore suppose that there is some definite number of electrons and protons in the world: theoretically a complete census would be possible."

How does that bear on the question of God's existence? Why, in this way. If the universe as a whole is limited, then it is made up of a limited number of parts. The number of parts may be greater than any we can ever definitely assign, but nevertheless it is limited. No matter how far we progress in splitting up matter, even if there are still smaller units than the protons and electrons, their number is limited. You cannot get infinity by dividing the finite.

But if the number of parts in the material universe is limited, then the number of combinations of those parts is limited. Probably you all remember in your school days in arithmetic or algebra dealing with formulas for calculating the number of different combinations possible for any given number of elements. If you know how many parts there are to start with, then you can calculate how many different combinations they can form.

Of course, in dealing with the whole universe we do not know how many parts there are. But since we do know—according to this modern scientific theory of relativity—that the number of parts is limited, we can legitimately conclude that the number of combinations between these parts is limited.

For a universe that has existed for only a limited period of time—no matter how many millions of years that may be—this does not create any difficulty. We are still forming new combinations among the various parts of the universe.

But this would be another matter for a universe that had existed for all eternity because eternity would be long enough to have exhausted all the possible combinations between the various parts of the universe. If the various elements of the universe have been changing their relations and entering into other combinations absolutely for all eternity, then the finite number of combinations must have been all gone through with.

We come, then, by a different scientific route to the same result as when considering evolution— that if the universe has actually existed for all eternity there has been a repetition of all the possible combinations between the various parts. As I said then, so I repeat now, in an eternally existing universe, just such a talk has been given to just such an audience innumerable times in the past.

Starting with one of the implications of this modern scientific theory of relativity, that the universe is finite, there is no way of escaping this difficulty of repetition if the universe has existed for all eternity.

It is possible to believe that we have had a repetition any number of times of all the possible combinations between the various parts of the universe. And anyone who wishes to maintain the eternal existence of the universe while accepting this conclusion, is free to do so. But certainly he ought not to accuse theists of credulity when he is willing to swallow any such belief himself. I can see some difficulties connected with a belief in God, but they are not nearly as serious as the difficulties inherent in the eternal existence of the universe. And if it is to be a choice between believing in God, and believing that there has been an indefinite repetition of all possible situations in this universe, then I choose God.

I hope that I have made fairly clear this difficulty confronting those who wish to do away with God. They are compelled to assert the eternal existence of the universe. And the eternal existence of the universe implies a repetition of all possible situations—including this very one in which we are now—if the universe is limited. And modern science, in the theory of relativity, holds that the universe is limited.

IV

Undoubtedly a considerable number of people think that science can explain the material universe apart from God. There is a story—whether true or not—attributed to a great astronomer, who when asked what became of God on his theory, replied: "I have no need for God!" But as a matter of fact, science, so far from doing away with the necessity of God, rather confirms this necessity by conjuring up difficulties in the way of an eternally existing universe.

We have just considered two such difficulties— one drawn from evolution, the other from relativity. Let us make it three of a kind by pointing out the bearing of the law of the diffusion of heat on an eternally existing universe.

You are all familiar with the experience of putting your hand on an iron railing on a cold day, and feeling the sensation of coldness. And contrariwise, you have also put your hand on the same rail after it has been exposed to the summer sun, and it has felt hot. This sensation of coldness or hotness comes from the fact that in the one case heat is passing from your hand to the rail, and in the other from the rail to your hand. Heat tends to diffuse itself. And so wherever there is a difference of temperature between two objects in close contact, there tends to be a passage of heat from the hotter to the colder.

And what we observe in our little world of experience, scientists tell us is going on all around us in the whole universe. The sun is radiating its heat, as is also the earth. According to astronomers our earth was once a molten mass that gradually cooled down to its present temperature. Lord Kelvin once calculated from the heat of the earth's interior that the earth was a certain number of million years old. That is to say, knowing the present condition of the earth, and the laws under which heat tends to be dissipated or diffused, he argued that it would have taken so many years to reach this state from the time it broke off from our sun.

Lord Kelvin may have been right or wrong by thousands or millions of years, but that does not affect our argument. The point is this: the present state of the earth implies a definite point of beginning. Two hundred million years—or two hundred billion years—is a sizable period of time, but it is not eternity. And this process of heat radiation could not have been going on for all eternity in the earth, or else it would have been completed. And what applies to our earth, applies to the universe as a whole. The universe is in a definite condition as regards heat, and that implies a definite point of beginning. For if the universe had been existing forever, eternally radiating heat, the tendency would have been realized of all bodies reaching the same temperature.

In the *Outline of Science,* edited by Professor Arthur J. Thomson, we read: "There must come a time, so far as we can see at present, when even if all the heat energy of the universe is not radiated away into empty infinite space, yet a uniform temperature will prevail. If one body is hotter than another, it radiates heat to that body until both are at the same temperature. . . . In this sense it may be said that the universe is running down" (p. 286).

From a philosophical standpoint, one can object to Professor Thomson speaking of infinite space, but passing over that, let us emphasize what Professor Thomson says as a scientist: that in this sense of all bodies tending to have the same temperature, the universe is running down. As long as we assume a limited period of time for the existence of the universe, this has no great significance. But it means a great deal against the theory of eternal existence for this universe. For if this tendency towards equalization of temperatures had actually been going on forever, everything would now be at the same temperature. The science of physics, therefore, in so far as it accepts as universally valid, this second law of thermodynamics, tends to prove that the universe must have existed for only a limited time, and therefore that the universe must have been created.

Perhaps we can go farther, as physicists, and say that the tendency of all bodies is to reach absolute zero. In the words of this same *Outline of Science:* "If all the molecules of a substance were brought to a standstill, that substance would be at absolute zero of temperature. There could be nothing colder. The temperature at which all molecular motion would cease is known: it is —273 degrees C. No body could possibly attain a lower temperature than this: a lower temperature could not exist."

And now note what Professor Thomson adds: "Unless there exists in nature some process, of which we know nothing at present, whereby energy is renewed, our solar system must one day sink to this absolute zero of temperature. The sun, the earth, and every other body in the universe is steadily radiating heat, and this radiation cannot go on forever, because heat continually tends to diffuse and equalize temperatures" (p. 287).

As a scientist Professor Thomson says this radiation cannot go on forever without reaching zero. But if eternal existence means anything, then it would have been going on forever had the universe existed from all eternity. Consequently—since we have not yet reached this absolute zero of temperature—the universe has not existed for all eternity.

It is possible, I admit, to conceive of some way by which this tendency towards zero could be offset. In a finite spheroidal universe, such as seems to be implied by the theory of relativity, heat might be reflected back from the spheroidal surface of the universe and focused upon some point or points. The result might be the kindling of new conflagrations, a starting over again of the process by which the universe evolved from a primal fire mist. But in that case we get back to our old difficulty of repetition. In an absolute eternity, this would have happened not only once but an indefinite number of times. Up through the various stages of evolution would have crept the universe, to be dissolved again in fire.

Certainly there is no evidence of such repetition. It is a belief, not a scientific fact. And there are no arguments for such a belief at all comparable to the arguments for a belief in God.

The tendency of science, indeed, may be to eliminate certain anthropomorphic ideas of God; it may be to carry over into the realm of orderly law what some primitive peoples have attributed to direct action by God; but the tendency of science is not to eliminate God altogether. On the contrary, science tends to make God more and more necessary. That is, the discovery of certain scientific laws or theories, such as evolution, relativity, the diffusion of heat, tends to show that the universe cannot have existed for all eternity. And if it has not existed for all eternity, then it must have been created. And if it has been created, then we have God.

v

The difficulties of the atheistic position which we have so far considered have been drawn from the field of science. But there are other difficulties as well, and I want you to go on with me to consider one of them. I shall approach the difficulty in a roundabout way, however, by asking you to remember that no matter what kind of radio receiving sets you happen to have, there are some sets made now to operate from the electric light current. And you know, also, that we have two kinds of electric current—direct and alternating. Some sets are made to use direct current, some to use alternating current. They are not interchangeable. You can use a set only with the current for which it was designed.

Most of you, I suppose, drive cars. And for those cars you use gasoline as a fuel. It would be possible to use alcohol, but that would require an engine or a carburetor of a somewhat different design. Alcohol can be adapted to the principle on which an internal combustion engine works, but you cannot use it right off in an automobile intended for gasoline. That is to say, engines are designed to operate under certain conditions, and we must recognize that fact if we are to get results.

Now, of course, I might go on piling up illustrations of machines designed in this machine age for one purpose or another. But these two examples—of the radio and the automobile—are sufficient to give us an idea of what is meant by design. We can define design as the intelligent adaptation of means to an end. In the examples I have given you, there was the adaptation of the various parts of the engine to the use of gasoline or alcohol, or of a radio set to a particular kind of current.

The men who designed these machines had a knowledge of certain principles, and of the way in which various materials act under certain circumstances, and they adapted these materials to the purpose they had in mind—the use of alternating current in a receiving set, or the use of gasoline for an internal combustion engine and the development of power. Everybody admits the existence of design here. It is the commonest thing in the world to speak of a machine being "designed" for a certain purpose. No sane man would think of denying design. If he said there was no such thing as design, of an inventor having a purpose in mind, he would simply convict himself of being mentally off.

No scientist would ever deny that the latest Ford car had a designer. He knows that engineers worked for months on the problem before them. If some professor of physics or astronomy or psychology or biology told his class they were laboring under a delusion in imagining that the car had a designer, that this was simply an outworn superstition of the Victorian era, they would laugh at him. They know better.

But if this is true of the Ford car, of a radio set, of a watch, and of every other mechanical invention, it is equally true of the universe as a whole, and of all the marvelous living machines we see around us. The ears with which you hear show just as much adaptation of means to an end as the receiving set invented by some human being; the lungs and larynx and all the rest of the body by which the voice is produced, need an inventor, a designer, just as much as an Edison phonograph.

Living machines are much more wonderful than any dead machines we human beings can make. The fact that they are alive, and able to reproduce themselves, does not do away with the necessity of a Designer. All that only makes the powers of the Designer so much the greater. If Mr. Ford instead of putting up his enormous factories for the manufacture of new Fords, had been able to design a car that would of itself produce new cars, he would be a much greater inventor than he is.

But no one would say that for this reason Mr. Ford was unnecessary to start the whole process.

Nor does the theory of evolution eliminate in any way the need of an inventor. If Mr. Ford could design a car that would not only reproduce itself, but would from time to time improve upon itself, would develop new features, and, as it were, meet the struggle for existence with other cars, this would be more wonderful still. Instead of doing away with Mr. Ford, it would increase his skill as a designer.

Now it follows very clearly from this, it seems to me, that the very much greater adaptation of means to ends that we see in the universe around us implies a Designer. There can be no machine without a mechanic. And to admit this in regard to the comparatively unimportant machines like automobiles and phonographs, and then to deny it in regard to the most important machine of all, the whole universe, is certainly to put a strain on our credulity.

All the talk in the world about Nature with a capital N, unknown forces, original nebulæ, protoplasmic slime, and all the rest, can never do away with the need of a Designer. The scientific discoveries of the last century have no more than emphasized this. The more science demonstrates the reign of law in nature, the more science ferrets out the principle of causality, the more emphatically does science point to some Lawgiver, some First Cause, some Being who designed the universe to operate in just the way it does. Science has not made a Designer unnecessary. On the contrary, science has made a Designer more necessary.

I have said that if one admits the need of a designer for a Ford car, he must logically admit a Designer for the universe as a whole. But the argument can be turned around, too. If one denies a Designer for the universe, then he must logically deny a designer for a Ford car. For there would be no place at which design could enter. If solar systems and oak trees and amœbas and monkeys are merely the result of blind forces, with no element of design, then men, too, are simply the result of blind forces. In that case, everything that men do is also the result of blind forces. There is no room for freedom of choice or for intelligence.

The reason for this is the principle of causality, on which the whole of modern science is built. Briefly, the principle of causality is that nothing in this world merely "happens." Everything has a cause. And the effect can never be greater than the cause. Whatever is in the effect is in the cause. Consequently, if there is design in the effect, there must have been design in the cause. And vice versa, if there is no design in the cause, then there can be no design in the effect.

Now the Ford car is an effect of a long series of causes. If there is design shown by this car, then there must be design in the causes. The design cannot be simply in Mr. Ford. For he, too, is an effect. If he has design, then his cause must have had design also. And just as the design of a Ford car implies a designer, so the design of Mr. Ford, and of the universe generally, implies a Designer. There is no way of getting out of this except by throwing overboard all science and all reason. You all have seen a magician on the stage draw rabbits out of a hat. Perhaps as children, you thought he was actually making rabbits out of thin air; just as certain backward races, without our knowledge of science, might believe. But as grown-ups, with a sophisticated, scientific attitude towards life, you know that a magician can only pull out of a hat what has been put into it. The fact that you did not see him put in the rabbits does not in the least alter your conviction.

Well, the same thing applies all along the line. No rabbits to begin with, then no rabbits at the end; rabbits at the end, then rabbits at the beginning. No design or Designer to begin with, then no design or designer at the end; design or a designer at the end, then design and a Designer at the beginning. If you admit design now in the automobiles, in receiving sets, in shotguns, in every invention of science—then you have to admit design in the human eye, in the dog's scent, in the bird's wings. And contrariwise, if you deny design at the beginning, you must deny design now. Otherwise, you will be a real magician, you will be pulling rabbits out of the hat when no rabbits have ever been put in there.

That is what a denial of an intelligent Creator for the universe brings us to. Instead of being scientific, it is leading us back to the days of magic. It is undermining all science because it is asserting that some effects had no causes, or that you can have an effect greater than its cause. It is getting something from nothing.

There are people who balk at creation, at the concept of a self-existent spiritual Being bringing matter into existence. But that is easy of acceptance beside the other alternative of matter without intelligence of itself bringing intelligence into existence; of matter without any design bringing into existence machines showing design.

Possibly a man can really believe that if he tries. But the majority of people find theism less of a strain on their credulity than atheism. And certainly the man who believes in this magic of the effect being greater than the cause, of pulling rabbits out of a hat when no rabbits have been put in, has no right to pose as intellectually superior, as more reasonable, than the theist.

Put in a perfectly definite, concrete way, the atheist says: Yes, I can get rabbits out of a hat without having put any rabbits in there. And the theist says: If rabbits are taken out of a hat, then they must have been there before.

III. ARGUMENTS FOR THE EXISTENCE OF GOD

Impossibility of infinite series of dependent causes; contingent beings imply a necessary Being; conscience based on a Supreme Being; on atheistic assumption no morality; the blankness of life without God.

III. ARGUMENTS FOR THE EXISTENCE OF GOD

I

YOUR attention has been called to certain difficulties connected with a denial of God's existence. But the case for theism does not rest upon the negative basis of the difficulties of atheism. It is not merely the choice of the less objectionable position from an intellectual standpoint. There are very solid arguments in favor of theism, and a consideration of at least some of these arguments is more than justified.

Of course, there is a difference in the appeal of different arguments to different individuals. But probably the best argument for theism with which to begin is the argument from causation. The whole of modern science presupposes the principle of causality. Every effect must have a cause. Nothing merely happens haphazardly without anything having caused it. Everything proceeds in an orderly way. The oak comes from an acorn, and not from a walnut; the chicken comes from an egg of one sort, a duck from another.

Back beyond the myriad of living things we see around us was a condition of simpler forms, so scientists tell us. Evolution implies the development of all these species from a very few earlier species. But evolution does not do away with the principle of causality, and is not itself a cause of the development. Each subsequent situation was contained in some way in the previous one. Indeed, evolution presupposes involution. Lengthening a pen does not enable it to write of itself.

And if going back beyond the present species does not do away with the need of causes operating to produce the present forms, so going back to the very simplest origins of protoplasm or fire mist does not do away with the need of a cause. Back through the period when animal life had not yet developed, past the first rudimentary forms of plants, to the time when this earth was a molten mass unfit for any living habitation, the principle of causality still held good. Each subsequent effect had a previous cause.

Beyond that, again, to the time before this earth of ours had split off from its parent sun, we can trace the law of cause and effect. We trail it up to the very beginning, whatever that may have been. No matter how long the series of causes, each effect must have had its appropriate cause. There is no room for chance to enter into this scientific world.

Primitive, unscientific folk might be satisfied with saying that the earth was supported by a gigantic elephant, and the elephant in turn by a tortoise. But we must go farther than that. We must ask what supported the tortoise. And ultimately we come to some first cause responsible for all the others.

A man cannot lift himself by his bootstraps. You cannot throw a chain up into the air and suspend it from nothing. If Archimedes is to move the earth with a lever, then he must have some fulcrum on which to rest it. From what does this series of causes we have traced in the universe start? What is the fulcrum from which the solar system is moved? A series of causes, each of which is dependent for its own being upon the cause just above it, cannot be infinite. We come ultimately to a First Cause, which is itself uncaused and independent.

That cause we call God. And while the argument I have used in its bareness does not prove that this First Cause is personal with any particular interest in us as individuals, this is because we cannot prove everything at once. Just now we must be content with showing that there cannot be an infinite series of dependent causes. In the future I shall go on to a consideration of the attributes of this First Cause.

You will note that I have said that there cannot be an infinite series of *dependent* causes. Personally, it seems to me that there cannot be an infinite series, or number, because series or number implies limitation, and the term infinite implies the limitless. But I know that mathematicians speak of infinite series, whether or not they mean this in a strict metaphysical sense. And so I prescind from the question of whether or not an infinite series is possible. The argument is restricted to the impossibility of an infinite series of dependent causes. There would never be any results from an infinite series of such causes. And since we have the obvious result in this world of ours, we know that the series of causes producing it cannot have been infinite.

A homely illustration from a nursery rime may serve to bring this out more clearly. You all remember the story of the house that Jack built, and how each time the story is repeated you add another item. This is the cow that gives the milk that feeds the man who lives in the house that Jack built; this is the maid who milks the cow that gives the milk that feeds the man who lives in the house that Jack built; this is the boy who kissed the maid who milks the cow that gives the milk that feeds the man who lives in the house that Jack built; and so on indefinitely.

The man would have a house to live in, and he could get his milk even if the boy had not kissed the maid who milks the cow. But this is because each item in the series is independent of the other. This is not a series of dependent causes. The maid did not milk the cow because the boy kissed her; and Jack would have had a house even if the maid had not milked the cow.

Let us, however, modify the story sufficiently to make each item dependent on the preceding, so that we do have a series of subordinate causes. This is the house that Jack built, begins it as before. But then we go on: These are the nails that joined the timbers that formed the house that Jack built; this is the hammer that drove the nails that joined the timbers that formed the house that Jack built; this is the wood that formed the handle of the hammer that drove the nails; this is the tree that gave the wood that made the handle of the hammer that drove the nails.

It ought to be evident that if we keep on adding a cause in an infinite series on which all subsequent causes are dependent, that there would never be any house, because there would never be any beginning of the series. I stopped arbitrarily at the tree. But the tree was dependent upon an acorn, and that acorn on another tree. If there was no beginning of that series, then there is no end, either. The whole thing is suspended in the air. Once you suppose a beginning, however, you have abandoned the idea of infinite. You have placed a definite limit.

Another illustration has often been used to bring out the difference between an infinite series of dependent causes and an infinite series of independent causes. A clock runs because of force coming from a coiled spring. If you assume that the clock has been rewound an infinite number of times, then you have an infinite series of independent causes. That would correspond to the assumption that an independent Being had created the world from all eternity. As far as our present argument is concerned, we care nothing about such an assumption one way or the other.

To get an analogy between the clock and our argument, it is necessary to prescind from the question of who winds the clock. The force from the coiled spring is applied through a series of wheels to the hands. Now suppose that instead of the half dozen or so wheels between the spring and the hands, there was an infinite series of wheels. You would never get back to the spring. A million wheels, a billion wheels, a quadrillion wheels is not an infinite series. Every time you thought you had finally reached the last wheel in the series, some logician would say: Not at all. An infinite series is larger than that.

It is clear that such a series of wheels is closed at one end by the hands of the clock. Now if it is an infinite series of wheels, it cannot be closed at the other end, too, the end of the spring. For certainly a series that has two ends—a beginning and an end—is not infinite. But if it is open at the end of the spring, then the spring is never reached. The spring can never exert any power on the last wheel—because there is no last in an infinite series —and consequently it can never move the hands. There is only a phantom clock.

Now if we have a real clock that actually runs, we know that the series of wheels between the hands and the clock is really not infinite. There is just a definite number of wheels.

And similarly, if we have not a phantom universe, but a universe that actually runs, we know that the series of dependent causes to account for the running, must be finite. The series can be a great deal longer than we can have in the series of wheels in a running clock, but the series cannot be actually infinite. You have to get back to the spring ultimately.

That spring corresponds, roughly, to the First Cause. And so we say that back of this going universe of ours there must be a First Cause. I am not concerned just now with the attributes of this First Cause. Our argument does not undertake to show whether it is personal or impersonal, material or spiritual, intelligent or non-intelligent, free or determined. All these considerations will have to wait. All that it is necessary to do now is to drive home the idea that there cannot be an infinite series of dependent causes; and that consequently there must have been a First Cause for the series of dependent causes we see operating in the universe around us.

II

A variation of the argument for the First Cause, is the argument from contingent beings. But though essentially the same as the First Cause argument, the contingent being argument lends some strength and persuasiveness. It is like putting flesh and bones on a skeleton. To fill out is to render attractive.

The idea of contingent beings is perfectly familiar, for a contingent being is simply one that does not have to exist of necessity. There is nothing in its nature that demands existence. It may exist or may not exist. Only a contingent being could indulge in the choice proposed by Hamlet's famous soliloquy, to be or not to be.

Contingent beings are all around us. In fact, they are the only beings we know directly. The hats we wear, the cigarettes we smoke, the beefsteak we eat, the cars we drive, are all contingent. We ourselves are contingent beings. There was a time when we were not. Our coming into existence depended upon a great multiplicity of factors. And everything else that we know, in this material world, is in a similar situation.

But contrasted with contingent beings, we can

logically conceive of a necessary being. The idea of a necessary being is not as familiar as the idea of a contingent being, because it is so different from ourselves. But with a little reflection we can easily see that the general category of being can be divided into necessary being and contingent being. A necessary being is a being whose very nature demands existence. It is incapable of not existing. And as a conclusion from that, we can say that a necessary being does not owe its existence to any other being. It is its own explanation. For if it were caused by some other being, then it would really be contingent, for its existence would be contingent upon the activity of that other being. Its own nature would not be such that it had to exist.

But not only can we conceive of a necessary being as contrasted with contingent beings. We can infer that the existence of contingent beings implies the existence of such a necessary being. And the reason is that no contingent being contains within itself the complete explanation of its own existence. It is contingent, and therefore dependent upon something else. My existence depends upon my parents, theirs upon my grandparents, and so on. The mere multiplication of the series does not explain it. There is always contingency, always dependency.

I may get back in tracing my ancestry to some Adamic amœba, or to a lifeless clod. But although a long ancestry may be self-sufficient for geneologists, it is not self-sufficient for logicians. Every step in the series is contingent, and consequently the whole is contingent. Merely multiplying contingent beings will never get anything but contingent beings. Consequently contingent beings can never explain their own existence.

Contingency is not simply something less than necessity, as a cent is something less than a quadrillion dollars, so that if only you have enough contingency you finally get necessity. On the contrary, contingency and necessity are by nature opposed, so that the more contingent a being is, the less necessary it is. And we may even say that the more contingent beings there are, the more need for some being that is not contingent, but necessary, to explain the existence of the contingent beings.

No logical legerdemain can escape from this conclusion. Anything else would be like the eastern serpent represented with his tail in his mouth. Where does the serpent come from? Out of his

[91]

own mouth! Where does the contingent being come from? From contingency! It is even worse than arguing: an apple is one-fiftieth as heavy as a watermelon, therefore, by adding together fifty apples you get a watermelon. If you multiply apples, you still have apples. And if you multiply contingency, you still have contingency.

The necessary being that must underlie all contingent beings is no other than what we have already called the First Cause, itself uncaused, itself not contingent, but necessary, absolutely distinct in essence from all contingent beings.

Of course there have been attempts to avoid this rigorous conclusion. One attempt is to extend the material universe to infinity as regards space and time, and so to make the boundary between the necessary and the contingent appear less sharp. But that does not really avoid the difficulty. For if each individual of the collective whole is itself contingent, then the whole is contingent. And certainly our observation proves that each being that we know in this material universe is itself contingent. In fact, contingent beings are the only ones that we know directly.

The materialist would take this line of thought. He would contend that though all particular individual material things are contingent, there is some sort of material substratum out of which they arose that is itself necessary. The particular manifestation is contingent, continually changing, evanescent, but not so the universal and eternal substratum of matter. But apart from the difficulty of design on any such basis, of morality, and of all the other difficulties, which we have already considered, there is the metaphysical difficulty. Why should this material substratum receive some perfections at one time, and other perfections at a different time? Matter can be a diamond, or a tree, or a man. The varying perfections of these different beings is not essential to matter. For what is essential and necessary is inseparable from it, and we know that these perfections are not inseparable. If they are not essential, then they must come from some eternal cause. When I fold a piece of paper into a triangle, I have conferred that form upon it. The form did not come of itself. A cause external to the paper had to produce it.

But if matter were really necessary being, no contingent being could confer any perfections upon it. For what is necessary can never receive perfection from what is not necessary. The necessary being can bring the contingent being into existence, but it is a contradiction to assert that the contingent can bring the necessary into existence. But this perfection, whatever it is, would, on the assumption of the materialists, be part of the necessary being, and so we should have the contradiction of the contingent, itself dependent upon the necessary, in its turn being the cause of part of the necessary. And if the contingent owes its whole existence to the necessary, what has it that it can give to the necessary?

Moreover, when we get back to the ultimate substratum of matter that materialists talk about, what is it? If it is the necessary being, then it exists of necessity. And if it changes to take on new perfections, or different perfections, what causes the change? Nothing in itself, for what it has in itself is necessary, and consequently could not have been nonexistent previously. But if the cause of the change comes from outside, then you have the logical contradiction of the contingent giving something to the necessary.

Another way out of the difficulty is attempted by some through the door of pantheism. That is the contention that contingent beings are merely modes of the one Absolute. They are manifestations of the necessary being, themselves not distinct, though dependent, beings. This Absolute is not material, it may even be personal, and consequently the system cannot be called materialistic. But it has the same logical flaw that materialism has.

The contingent beings we know, whether they are manifestations of the one Absolute or of a material substratum that is nameless, are constantly changing. And in their changes they are acquiring new perfections. These new perfections must come from some outside agent. And if they have no separate existence from the Absolute, then the Absolute is really the recipient of new perfections. Once more we have the necessary receiving something from the contingent.

Consideration of contingent beings leads us back inevitably to the necessary being. And the necessary being is merely the philosopher's name for God. For the necessary being must possess at least all the perfections we find in contingent beings, and personality is one of those perfections.

III

The fact of dependent contingent beings leads back inexorably to a necessary First Cause. And

[95]

the actual universal existence of conscience, as some sense of right and wrong, can legitimately be appealed to as proving the existence of some Person back of the whole process. For if there is such a thing as conscience, a consciousness of responsibility, a distinction between moral right and wrong, it can be only on the basis of some Being to whom one is responsible.

And if we understand just what is meant, the universal existence of conscience can hardly be denied. We do not mean that all persons have exactly the same moral code, but only that they have some code. Everyone, broadly speaking, looks upon at least some things as morally wrong.

There are individuals, it is true, who sometimes claim to have no moral sense whatever. And undoubtedly they have no qualms of conscience in doing certain things forbidden by the ordinary code of society. Now and then, for instance, we have the case of a Leopold and Loeb, or of a Hickman. But whether or not these particular individuals felt no compunction for what they did, I think we are safe in saying that their conduct shocked all but an infinitesimal portion of the population. On the theory that there is no morality, no God, no Lawgiver, then what they did is in essence no different

[96]

from what a butcher does in cutting up a steer. Very few, however, are willing to drive that theory to such a conclusion.

And even if Leopold and Loeb and Hickman, together with a small number in the population, have no moral sense, may not that be due to some defect in them? There are mental defects, all the way from idiocy to lack of talent in certain directions. And may there not be corresponding defects in the emotional make-up and in the moral sense? The existence of a few individuals devoid of all moral sense really proves nothing against the fact that the vast majority of the human race does have such a sense.

Nor does it make any difference to the argument that the content of this sense varies from time to time, and even among individuals. The essential point is that practically all men realize that for them some actions are morally wrong, others morally right. They may be like the old Scottish brigand in one of Walter Scott's tales, who felt at liberty to break every oath except one sworn on the handle of a favorite dagger. The possession of a moral sense about even one thing, no matter how grotesque in the estimate of society, is sufficient for our argument.

Starting, then, with the fact of a universal moral sense, we ask whence came this moral sense? How did this conviction originate? On what is it based?

And the answer is that the universal existence of a moral sense presupposes the existence of God. For without God, there would be a purely mechanical evolution. There would be nothing from which a moral sense could evolve. The factors in the situation would inexorably work out against any moral sense whatever. If what we think is inevitably determined by mechanical laws, then these laws should work out a conviction of mechanism. The very fact that they have worked out a universal conviction of something beyond the mechanistic is in itself a proof that mechanism is not a complete explanation. Anyone who disputes this should try to show how purely mechanical factors, x, y, z, can produce something that is a contradiction of the purely mechanical.

Mill and others have tried to get around the difficulty by reducing all morality to a question of expediency. But that morality is something more than expediency will be clear to anyone who tries to impose a moral obligation upon others by arguments ignoring God. He may, perhaps, con-

[98]

vince himself. But with others he will have no success.

To make matters concrete, let us take a definite situation. Suppose that David has satisfied his desire for the wife of Uriah, and the Prophet Nathan undertakes to convince him of sin. But instead of starting with the common belief in God, neither David nor Nathan have any use for such a supposition. How would Nathan go about his task?

Well, Nathan might point out that such conduct was against the tribal customs, that David could afford to be satisfied with what he already had, that such love affairs are temporary and never lead to real happiness, that all the men surrounding David would now be fearful of some such aggression against themselves, and that David was weakening their political loyalty. But all of these arguments are based upon expediency. None of them assume a moral sense, a conscience, in David. And consequently none of them are an explanation for the fact of David's having a moral sense. They would never produce in David the reaction that the Book of Kings records, the conviction of sin, and remorse, and repentance.

David, of course, traced his moral sense back

to the existence of God. His conscience was not very delicate in some directions, and in others he allowed passion to over-rule it. Nevertheless, he did have a conscience of a sort. And nearly everybody else has a conscience, too. Their conscience, like David's, is based in the last analysis, on God. Logically, if we eliminate God, we eliminate a moral sense, a conscience, from humanity. And, contrariwise, as long as we have conscience, we have the logical demand for God, for a Lawgiver, for some Person to whom the conscience is responsible. On the evolutionary supposition that any given situation really was contained in the previous situation, God must have been in order that a sense of morality should be evolved.

God and conscience go together. You cannot have one without the other. You cannot do away with one without doing away with the other. Consequently, the atheist, to be logical, must deny any moral difference between lighting a cigarette and lighting a human torch soaked in gasoline at some lynching bee. And the atheist must explain, on his own purely mechanical principles, how conscience ever came from non-conscience.

IV

To be logical, the atheist must give up conscience and give up morality. That is a staggering difficulty on the supposition that there is no God. For as far as I can see there is no way of proving any such thing as moral right or wrong without God. That is to say, if there be no God, then there is no moral right and no moral wrong. Every action, no matter how revolting it is, would be on the same *moral* plane with every other action. For a child to kill its mother in order to get insurance would have no more moral quality than eating an ice cream cone.

There are serious enough difficulties connected with morality even for a theist. But they are as nothing compared with the difficulty of proving the existence of morality if God is ruled out. Morality implies God. Morality stands or falls with God. Let me see if I can make clear what brings me to this view.

We can divide into three classes the actions to which we apply the terms "right" and "wrong." First of all, we have some actions that are commanded or proscribed merely by the requirements of polite society. In this sense, we say it is wrong to eat peas with a knife. One may feel very embarrassed at using the wrong fork at a formal dinner, but the feeling is essentially different from remorse at some moral lapse. And while there are higher degrees in the social code, rising to a gentleman's sense of honor, or noblesse oblige, the difference is only of degree and not of kind.

Then there is, secondly, the class of actions commanded or forbidden by the civil law, and the civil law only. In themselves they are seen to have no moral bearing. Examples of such actions would be driving past a traffic signal, or using the American flag for advertising purposes. Here, too, no sense of moral guilt attaches to the acts themselves. Whatever pricks of conscience come, arise from the fact that there is a moral obligation to obey the civil authority.

But there is a third group of actions to which we apply the terms "right" and "wrong." Those actions have a moral implication. They are a violation of something more than a mere social or legal code. I believe everyone recognizes in his innermost heart that murder is in a different category from cutting lettuce with a knife, or crossing a street when the traffic signals are against one. Even those who would deny any such thing as sin would probably feel that murder is breaking a different kind of prohibition than a merely social or legal prohibition. It is not a question of degree only, of the seriousness of the action. It is a matter of kind. Moral right and wrong are essentially different from what is merely socially or legally wrong. What is morally wrong may be forbidden by polite society and by the civil law, or it may not be so forbidden. Its quality of moral wrongness comes from something other than social custom or the enactments of the State.

What is the essence of this difference? Moral right and wrong, unlike merely social or legal right and wrong, bring us into a special relationship with a person to whom we are responsible. There must be a person, and there must be responsibility.

It is true that the moral code differs from age to age, and from people to people. It is also true, probably, that what was at one time merely a social custom has come in particular instances to be looked upon as having a moral character. But this does not do away with the difference between the moral and the merely social. For if the moral and the social were the same, then all social customs would be looked upon as moral. All that this suggestion explains is how some particular acts came to be looked upon as moral. It does not explain how there was a category of "moral" to which certain social customs could be transferred and thereby given greater sanction.

That greater sanction implies a reference to a personal Being. And that personal Being must be over the individual. It is true that violating the rights of another person, even though that person be merely one's equal, puts such an act in a different class from mere bad manners. But how comes it if all are equal, that one individual has rights against another? If there is no Superior to whom all equal human individuals are responsible, then I find it impossible to fix a moral obligation. Morality vanishes into thin air.

The essence of morality I can find only in relationship to that superior personality. If the idea of a personal Being, above all human beings, is taken away, then I see nothing left really to distinguish morally right or wrong actions from those only socially or legally right or wrong. There is the same kind of reason, and no other, for avoiding murder or perjury, as there is for avoiding what is looked upon as ill-bred. The reason may be greater, but it does not differ in kind.

Study the matter as hard as I can, I do not find any convincing argument for compelling people to refrain from these acts classified as morally wrong if there is no God, and they can get away with it. I may say that everyone should respect the personality of everyone else, and that all these morally wrong acts in some way violate personality. But when an objector replies: "Why should I respect the personality of someone else, when that someone else has not respected my personality? If he has injured me, why should I not revenge myself?", I have no answer that does not demand God. Without God, I have to admit there is no logical reason to restrain one—except, of course, fear of the consequences.

Moreover, each one of us is a person just as much as anyone else is. And when anyone's personal development comes into conflict with another's personal development, which should be the one to yield? If there is no God, then there is nothing higher than the individual human personality. Each individual is supreme. In a sense he is sovereign, and no one may place a moral obligation upon him to cramp his own development because it would interfere in some way with that of another.

[105]

I cannot say that these actions which are labeled immoral are so because they invade the rights of others, if there is no God, for God is the only solid basis for any rights. I find no logical way of vindicating my rights against another except it be through some higher personality. If there is no higher personality, my rights are lost.

And consequently the whole system of morality collapses if God is denied. There is left only the unrestrained struggle of sovereign individuals, except in so far as they are held in check by the sanctions of law or of public opinion. I have to acknowledge that the men who deny God and then speak about self-expression and self-development at the expense of our traditional moral code are at least logical. They have denied God, and they follow this position out to its logical consequences of denying all morality. On their assumption each individual may do as he thinks necessary for the development of his own personality, for the reaping of the greatest variety and intensity of experiences.

It would be untrue to say that all who deny the existence of God lead such unrestrained lives. On the contrary, the lives of many unbelievers are better and nobler—from a moral standpoint—

than the lives of many believers. But I am convinced that the reason for this is that they have absorbed a great deal from a religious atmosphere. Our civilization is still largely religious. There is in this country no atheist who has been brought up in a completely atheistic environment. In spite of his professed atheism he will have been influenced somewhat by the religious ideas of those around him.

The exemplary lives of atheists do not alter the fact that there is no logical way of proving moral responsibility without God. And so those who hesitate to do away with all moral responsibility should face this difficulty squarely. They cannot eat their cake and keep it, they cannot deny God and have moral responsibility. And they should consider not only what are the lives and standards today of unbelievers, but what they would be if atheism became universal. There would remain the standards supplied by social custom, by civil law, but there would be no moral code.

Personally, I do not want to face such a condition. I want to keep my sense of moral responsibility, and I want others to keep theirs. The world is bad enough as it is. There is too much sin now, but I am afraid there would be a great deal more if everyone faced life on the conviction that there was no such thing as morality. Yet that would be a logical conclusion, as far as I can see, from a denial of God. To have morality we must have God as well.

v

Bishop Spalding once said that if the universe were but a cinder and life a hell, yet it would be good to know the fact. And while, strictly speaking, it is not an argument against atheism to show the general blankness of life without God, and especially the moral chaos, nevertheless it is good to face the picture.

On the supposition that there is no God, naturally there is no future life for any of us. We are no more than the dust to which our body crumbles on burial. Death ends everything. After the grave is a blank just as complete and impenetrable as the blank that preceded our birth. Instead of the joy which eye hath not seen, nor ear heard, nor heart of man conceived, there is complete unconsciousness.

To look forward to such annihilation, inevitably affects our present existence very intimately. For our outlook on life varies to a large extent with

[108]

our expectation of life. If our physician were to tell us that we had at most only a few months to live, we should face those months with a different attitude from what we should have had on the supposition that we should live for years. And the same thing holds, with the necessary difference, regarding an expectation of life beyond the grave.

There are some, of course, who react to this belief in annihilation by adopting the attitude, "Let us eat, drink and be merry, for tomorrow we die." And for a while that may satisfy them, because they really do not mean tomorrow. They mean ten years hence, twenty years hence, at some indefinite future, and they have simply driven the thought of death out of their minds by their eating and drinking. But when tomorrow comes actually to mean in twenty-four hours, that is quite a different matter. Then the thought of death can no longer be shoved aside. Instead of the prospect of eating and drinking, there is the yawning grave, and the normal human being revolts at the idea that this spells annihilation.

Moreover, this attitude assumes that we can eat and drink and be merry. But there are situations for all of us when this is impossible. If a man lives long enough there comes a time when physically he is unable to eat and drink and be merry; and there are many other times when because of some circumstances he cannot get himself into this frame of mind. The man whose whole fortune has just been swept away may not feel like eating and drinking; the man whose beloved wife or mother or child has just been buried does not feel like eating and drinking and making merry, unless he is a brute. And there are always large percentages in our industrial civilization who have not the wherewithal to eat and drink merrily.

When you come to analyze it, you find that atheism is a fair weather philosophy. But life has its squalls and tempests as well as its sunshine. Atheism has but sorry comfort to offer when the sun of life is overclouded. It does not stand up against all the circumstances of life for all groups of humanity. There comes a time for everyone when it fails to satisfy. For the atheist has none of the consolations that come from belief in a future life. In the midst of his suffering, he cannot comfort himself with the thought of a compensating future.

Apart, however, from any need of evening up for pain and sorrow, there is an innate desire for immortality. And that desire cannot be satisfied by some sort of vicarious immortality through descendants who know nothing and care nothing about us. Nor will an evanescent fame of which we shall know nothing meet the demand. If we are not to live personally and individually, then life has tricked us. Nature has played a cruel joke upon her highest production. Man's end is frustration.

Again, if there be no God, then there is no such thing as free will. Later on we shall consider this question of human freedom more at length, but now I want at least to point out lack of freedom as one of the cumulative ill effects of atheism. For atheism destroys all human responsibility. If atheism be true, then we are on the same plane as the brute animals. As I said previously, on this supposition of atheism, there is no moral quality to any of our actions. To soak a woman's clothes in gasoline and set fire to her through spite is exactly the same—from a moral standpoint—as lighting a cigarette. For there is no morality without God.

And if there be no responsibility, then there is no personality. We are all as much automata as the mechanical man the newspapers have recently told us about. If there be no personal God, then our own personality shrinks and shrivels to the dimensions of a mere machine.

Furthermore, if there be no God, then there is no prayer. There is no sense of contact with a superior being, no confidence of help in any of the circumstances of life. As the writer in the *Plain Talk* magazine said, we must be our own God. And she confessed that she was making rather a poor job of it. When you contrast that with the sublime confidence of spiritual souls, with the undaunted faith of the martyrs, with the steady facing of disaster by thousands of saintly folk today, certainly life seems blank indeed under atheism.

Besides the same arguments that were used further back to show there could be no morality under atheism, also show that there can be no solid basis for government. What right has any individual to set himself up above others as their ruler, unless this right is founded on the will of someone superior to all human beings? If there is no God, then we are all equal. Physical force may compel me to render obedience, but it is only physical force. There is no moral obligation, and if I am strong enough or clever enough to evade the law, I may do so. In fact, I may even force my will on others.

And while force may be effective in some particular cases, or for a limited time, no government can really endure on this basis. If there is not the conscience of the people back of the law, the government can never enforce it. In ultimate analysis all governments depend upon a moral right. This is shown quite clearly in regard to prohibition. In those sections where the people generally are opposed to the law, and feel no obligation in conscience to obey it, the government is powerless. This moral basis for law does not mean that God picks an individual ruler and confers authority upon him, as in the old theory of the divine right of kings. But it does mean that some superior Being so designed men that they had to live in society and had to have some authority over them. On any other supposition there is no authority, but only force.

Without God, then, there would be no morality, no consolation derived from belief in a future life, no support from prayer, no sound basis for government. Life would be a hopeless chaos, a blank despair, at least at times. All these considerations are cumulative. Each one adds to the weight of the others. The sum total for anyone who considers them carefully ought to be overwhelming.

And in addition to all this, there are the intellectual considerations I have been pointing out. To deny God is equivalent to affirming the eternal existence of this material universe. And to assert the eternal existence of a material universe raises difficulties from the standpoint of evolution, from the finiteness of the universe—as implied by the theory of relativity—and in regard to the law of the diffusion of heat.

From all three of these standpoints, either the material universe has not existed for all eternity, or else there has been repetition. And repetition is so much more difficult to believe than theism, that it would seem only reasonable to choose theism.

But this is not the whole case for theism. There are not only difficulties in the way of atheism, but there are very solid, positive arguments in favor of theism, proving that there must have been a necessary personal First Cause to explain the existence of dependent, contingent persons with a sense of moral responsibility. And it might be added that there are no such positive arguments in favor of atheism. The man who undertakes to prove that there is no God has an impossible task.

IV. THE NATURE OF GOD AND HIS RELATIONS TO HIS CREATURES

God's eternity; His foreknowledge; His omnipresence; the problem of reconciling evil with God's goodness; prayer and miracles; the "how" of creation.

IV. THE NATURE OF GOD AND HIS RELATIONS TO HIS CREATURES

I

So far we have been concerned only with showing that the material universe which we know does not explain itself. There must have been some power outside of it to bring it into existence. As Dr. Kirtley F. Mather, professor of geology in Harvard, writes in his recent book *Science in Search of God*, "There is 'something back of the universe.' Matter is neither eternal nor ultimate; it is a temporary and local expression of energy" (N. Y., Henry Holt, 1928, p. 65). Then he goes on to say that science tells us this something back of the universe is a spirit and a person.

We can pass over the question whether it is science or philosophy that is making this particular contribution to our knowledge of what is back of the universe. The significant thing is that a professor of a physical science such as geology, in a university such as Harvard, should make this statement. And though perhaps not strictly within the field of scientific research, the statement that

God is a spirit and a person is nevertheless as certain as anything in science.

For the whole of science is based on the principle of causality. Every effect must have had a cause, and a cause proportionate to the result. There can be nothing in the result that was not contained implicitly in its antecedents. If there could be something in the effect that was not in the cause—at least implicitly—then that something would be uncaused. And if there can be something happening now without any cause, there can be no science. We would be living in a world of magic, instead of in a world of uniformity.

Now we experience in ourselves two powers that go to make up human personality—intelligence and freedom. I know, of course, that the existence of freedom is denied by some philosophers and by some scientists. We shall come to that later. But whatever it is that makes human personality must in some way be in the First Cause. Even now for the sake of convenience, I shall call these attributes intelligence and freedom. In short, God knows and God wills.

Moreover, as Professor Mather remarked, matter is not eternal. And since this First Cause, God, must be eternal, He cannot be matter. Some philosophers have seen no contradiction in an eternally existing material universe, if it were created from eternity, but others do see such a difficulty. And from a scientific standpoint a space-time world seems to imply a limitation on the duration of existence. If, then, God is not material, He must be spiritual. Professor Mather says: "At last we are coming to see that he is spirit" (p. 72). What he means, undoubtedly, is that at last we are coming to see that science implies that the something back of this material universe is spiritual. For we have long known the spirituality of God by other means than physical science. Even the Greek philosophers had a knowledge that the First Cause was not material.

A being that through its own nature is infinite in any one direction, must be infinite in all directions. Consequently the First Cause, being infinite as to duration, must be infinite in every other way. He is infinite as to knowledge and as to power. The philosophic conception of God is that He knows all things—present, past and future; those that have happened or could have happened under different circumstances; those that are determined; and those that are the result of human freedom.

The way in which God knows all these things is another question. We must make God to some extent in our own image, by attributing to Him the highest attributes we have. But they are attributed only by analogy. We shall never understand God completely, because the finite can never contain the infinite. We are making God anthropomorphic in a sense, but in a perfectly legitimate sense. God must be made in some image. And surely the image of man, the highest creature we know is better for our purpose than the image of a cow or a cabbage or a stone. A god that was thoroughly comprehended by human minds would indeed be anthropomorphic—he would be a merely human creation. For the finite there must always be mysteries in the infinite.

However, a little light can be thrown on the question of God's eternal existence and His knowledge of things that happen in time, if we consider some speculations of the theory of relativity. Because we live in a space-time universe, there is for us, present, past and future. But what is present, past or future will depend upon the relative position of the observer. Consequently what is past for one observer may be future for another. A sort of trick illustration of this would be the fact that a man broadcasting in Rome, Italy, at seven a.m., November eighth, might be heard in Dodge City, Kansas, at ten p.m., November seventh.

Bertrand Russell in his book *The A B C of Relativity*, gives an example of how the "time" of anything is relative to the position of the hearer. He supposes that two gunmen on a train shoot the engineer in his caboose and a brakeman on the end of the train. At the court trial, a man in the center of the train testifies that he heard the shots simultaneously, whereas a stationmaster standing on a platform exactly midway between the two thugs testifies that he first heard the shot which killed the brakeman. Can both witnesses be right? Yes. And the reason is that they are in different relative positions.

Russell has another example. "Suppose," he says, "that I could observe a person in Sirius, and he could observe me. Anything which he does, and which I see before the event E occurs to me, is definitely before E; anything which he does after he has seen the event E is definitely after E. But anything that he does before he sees the event E, but so that I see it after the event E has happened, is not definitely before or after E" (p. 62).

[121]

Now these quotations are simply to show that "time" is a relative conception dependent upon our spatial world. The position in which we happen to be relatively to any event, determines the time for us. But the time may be different for one in a different relative position. What is past for us may be future for him. And that leads us to the possibility of God being in such a relation to the universe that there is no present, past or future for him, but only one eternal now. Consequently God knows acts that are future for us, but He does not foreknow future acts, because to Him they are not future. From such a standpoint, there would be no difficulty involved in God's knowing everything that occurs in this world of ours.

We must not, on the other hand, think of God as "outside" this universe. He is not in some far-away spot observing us from a distance. In fact, just as "time" in a certain sense does not exist for God, neither does space. God is immanent in this universe. He is everywhere in it. But He is not in it in the same way that spatial beings are in it. As a spirit, God has no parts, and consequently He is not in the universe through part of Him being in one place, and part of Him in another.

God is infinite in power, because He is the First Cause. He exists by necessity, of His very nature. Consequently, there is no being outside of God who could have limited Him, for all other beings owe their existence to Him. And there is nothing in the conception of a necessary being which would imply limitation. On the contrary, the nature of necessary Being implies no limitation.

In considering the unlimited power of God, however, we must avoid one rather obvious fallacy —that God can perform a contradiction. The omnipotence of God implies that He can do "anything." Note the word "anything." This "anything" does not include that which in itself is a contradiction. Such a contradiction would be "nothing" or "no thing." Hence God cannot make a square circle, because a square and a circle are mutually exclusive. He cannot make a thing be and not be at the same time under the same aspect. But this is not a limitation upon God's power. He is still all-powerful, or omnipotent, for He can do *anything*. These illustrations are "nothings."

Nor should God's omnipresence be confused with pantheism. God is everywhere, and so in each human being, but we are not parts of Him. He is with us and in us by His knowledge, His power, His essence, but it is in such a way as to make a perfect distinction between Himself and us. The God of the theist is not an absentee mechanic who has designed the universe and set it in motion, and is now paying no attention to it, but is busied with some far-off world. But neither is He the God of the pantheist, in whom the finite is identified with the infinite.

God is in His world, and the same power that He put forth in the beginning to create it, must be put forth every moment to sustain it. For just as a contingent being cannot be the cause of its own beginning, so it cannot be the cause of its own continuance. Contingency always remains contingency. Any contingent being would go back into the nothingness from which it came, unless it were sustained in existence by the Necessary Being.

The intimacy of this sustaining power of God that underlies the contingency of created things can hardly be exaggerated, except by pantheism. For contingent existence can never be independent existence. Consequently, I cannot so much as lift my little finger without God's power being put forth to enable me to do so. In strict philosophic literalness, we live and move and have our being in God.

II

The fact that God is intimately present to each individual human being, whether that individual ever thinks of God or not, deserves some further consideration.

First of all, God is present to us by His knowledge. He knows everything. And as a consequence, being infinitely perfect, and living in one eternal now, He knows us more intimately than we know ourselves. He knows everything that we have done, or shall do. He knows not only our external actions, but He also knows our innermost thoughts and aspirations. And God knows the motives under which we acted. Sometimes a man can deceive himself as to why he does a thing, and actually think that he is actuated by a high form of patriotism, for instance, when in reality a keener analysis would show the element of private gain. But a man cannot deceive God.

There is another way, too, in which God knows us better than we know ourselves. He is the Author of human nature. He knows its capacities in all directions, both good and bad. God knows that a particular individual who prides himself on his strength to resist the temptation to drink, let us say, or on never having had a temptation, is really going to be led on by imperceptible steps until he ends in the gutter. And on the other hand, God knows the unsuspected heroic capacity of certain other individuals. He knows that under the molding influences of the future, this man will develop out of his present selfishness into the highest type of unselfishness.

God knows us better than we know ourselves, because we are always limited to our own experience, and that experience is extremely narrow. We know to some extent what we are, or what we have been, but hardly at all what we shall be. We can never know human nature as the Author of that nature knows it. There will always be unsuspected depths, surprising flashes of power. What changing circumstances will bring about in ourselves, is known to God, but hidden from us.

Then, too, God is present to us not only by His knowledge, so that we cannot hide from His all-seeing eye—to speak figuratively—but He is also present to us by His power. Inasmuch as we are contingent beings, we depend ultimately upon some necessary Being for our creation, and our continued existence is still dependent upon that necessary Being. That is to say, the same power that brought us into existence must be constantly exerted, else we should go back into the nothingness from which we came. We have no more power to exist now of ourselves, than we had to exist of ourselves before this necessary Being brought us into existence.

We can coil a spring, and that spring will exert a certain pressure until it is uncoiled; or we can accumulate a certain amount of electric power in a storage battery. Because these materials continue to exist according to their particular natures, they will continue to exert this power. But the power of existing is much more fundamental. Existence must be given continuously by the same cause that operated originally to produce existence.

Man is not different in this respect from the spring or the storage battery. He has not been given power of existence once for all, so that he keeps on running, as it were. Man has not a certain supply of power that he can continue to use until that much is gone. There is, rather, a sort of constant drag back into nothingness, and that drag must be continuously, momently, overcome, if he is to keep on existing. And the only power that can overcome man's tendency to revert to nothingness is the power that created him.

Consequently, we cannot take a breath, or think a thought without the same intimate coöperation of God's power that was necessary to bring us into existence. The parents who are the natural instruments by which life is given to a child, have to protect and nourish the child if it is to live. But there comes a time, normally, when the child matures, and is able to live independently of its parents. No such time ever comes when we can live independently of God. Always we are much more intimately dependent upon God than even the unborn child is dependent upon its mother.

Let us frankly face the implications of theism in this direction. The man who, contrary to his mother's emphatic teaching, draws a revolver, pulls the trigger, and shoots an innocent man for the sake of robbery, is doing that by only the remotest sort of coöperation from his mother. She merely gave him life to start with. But he goes through each action necessary for this crime by the closest sort of physical coöperation from God. It is by God's power, put forth at that very moment, that he pulls the trigger. If God did not coöperate in that act, then he would not be able to move his finger, the trigger would remain unpulled, and no bullet would be sent upon its death-dealing path.

I know the tremendous difficulty that this makes for theism. Immediately the thought occurs: How can we reconcile this with an all-good, and an all-loving God? We shall consider that difficulty later. Now, I merely want to emphasize the intimateness of the coöperation between God and man, in order to show our complete dependence upon God.

And in addition to being present to us by His knowledge and by His power, God is present to us by His essence. God's power cannot be where He is not. As His power keeps us in existence, coöperates with every act of ours, God must be where those acts are taking place. God is not simply near us, as we are near a human friend. God is not simply around us, as the atmosphere surrounds our body. But God is interpenetrating every particle of us. There can never be as intimate a union between two human beings as that between ourselves and God.

So intimate, indeed, is this union that there is a sort of natural tendency towards pantheism among those who think a great deal about the union of God and His creatures. Even among Christian mystics, we find language that, strictly interpreted, would seem to be pantheistic. Thus Eckhardt writes: "Our Lord says to every living man, 'I became Man for you. If you do not become God for Me, you do Me wrong' " (Underhill, E., *Mysticism*, p. 502). And if the orthodoxy of Eckhardt be somewhat suspect, the same cannot be said of St. Augustine, who uses language just as strong: "I am the food of the full grown; grow and thou shalt feed on Me. Nor shalt thou change Me into thy substance, but thou shalt be changed into Mine" (*Confessions*, VII, 10; or Underhill, p. 502). And Catherine of Genoa says: "My being is God, not by simple participation, but by true transformation of my being" (Underhill, p. 153).

Of course, I am not accusing these mystics of being pantheists. I simply refer to their words in the effort to drive home to you the extreme intimacy of the union between God and yourselves.

A consideration of that intimacy can lead to two very different courses of thought. One, as I have already intimated, is the problem of evil. How can God permit, and even physically coöperate in so much pain and suffering and sin?

But the other, and the one now to be dwelt upon, is the dignity given to man by this union with God. We are indeed children of God in a much more true and intimate sense than we are children of our human parents, because God has not only given us existence in a much more fundamental way than they have done, but He has kept us in existence. And He has always been with us much more intimately than any human parent could ever be. And so we are temples of God, pure, holy, sanctified temples; or foul, unclean, desecrated ones, as we have willed.

III

The question of God's omniscience, omnipotence, and omnipresence, as I have said, lands us squarely in the most difficult problem of theism— the existence of evil, both physical and moral.

The merely rational solution of the problem of evil, especially of moral evil, leaves us unsatisfied. As regards physical evil, some have held that this is the best possible world, and that God could not have created a better one. But that is clearly to limit God's power, to give up His omnipotence. For there is no contradiction involved in arranging the world in such a way that there would be much less suffering than at present.

Others have blamed all physical evil on Original Sin. In the beginning, they say, there was no physical suffering, no death. These entered the world only because our first parents disobeyed God. Men suffer because they have been thus placed at odds with their Creator. But a very little reflection shows that this explanation simply pushes the problem back a step farther. Why did the first man to be tested in the name of the race fall into sin? If God is all-powerful and all-knowing, then He knew this individual would sin. He could have selected from all the possible human beings those who would not have disobeyed Him.

But although the merely rational answer to this problem leaves us unsatisfied, there is a practical solution—the acceptance of the fact of suffering. Though we do not know why, suffering seems to be a very deeply imbedded law in the universe. All Christians believe that Jesus submitted Himself to suffering for man's redemption. But one need not be a Christian to recognize that apparently we grow, or can grow, spiritually, by suffering. Strength of character is developed in adversity. Understanding and sympathy are born of the experience of suffering.

I do not mean by this that everybody always profits by suffering in growing spiritually. Some people are soured by suffering. They become worse instead of better. But it is probable, nevertheless, that most human beings are benefited by suffering. There is an old proverb that it is harder to stand prosperity than to stand adversity. Reviewing your own lives, can you not see that what was very painful at the time proved ultimately to be a source of character development? Your own dispositions have been improved and mellowed by sorrow and suffering. From the vantage point of experienced suffering, you can look back and see that at times you were cruel and callous and selfish because you had not suffered.

If you apply this test to other persons, the result is perhaps even clearer. Can you not check off, in imagination, a number of persons who are insufferable, because they never suffered? They would be much pleasanter companions if only pain and sorrow had rubbed off some of their angles, made them less cocksure of things, humbled their pride somewhat. They need the discipline of hard knocks. The choice souls are those who have shaken hands with disaster.

And taking the matter in a wide, objective way, does it not work out in the long run that the children of wealthy parents, shielded as much as possible from the hardships of life, come ultimately to be unable to meet life successfully? They go down in the struggle for existence because they have never developed stamina through suffering. They are flabby spiritually, because their spiritual muscles have never been stretched to the breaking point against adversity.

All this, of course, does not tell us why God designed suffering as a means of growth, when He might have arranged for the same strength of character in some other way. But it does point out what our attitude should be, since we are in a world where suffering conditions development. We ought deliberately and consciously to use suffering for this end. We ought to struggle against being soured and disgruntled because a few slings and arrows of outrageous fortune strike us. We ought to emulate those who have profited by suffering to become brave, sweet-tempered, calm in soul, in the face of the most adverse circumstances.

But after all, the problem of physical evil is relatively simple. The really baffling difficulty for the theist is the existence of moral evil, or sin. True, moral evil is sometimes used as an explanation of physical evil. And when the question is asked, why did an all-powerful, all-good God bring creatures into existence knowing that they would abuse their powers against Him, we are told that this is an essential accompaniment of free will.

But as a matter of fact, sin and free will do not necessarily go together. It is only the *possibility* of sinning that is necessary for freedom in this life of ours. No man commits all the sins he might commit. And just as men were created who would resist some temptations, so men could have been created who would have resisted all temptations. The moral trial and struggle of this life would not have been eliminated, but there would always have been victory.

Indeed, it can be contended that even the possibility of sinning is not essentially necessary for freedom. For the blessed in heaven are no longer subject to sin. Yet they have not for this reason been deprived of their freedom. An all-powerful

God, therefore, could have designed a universe in which free human beings would live and act, but in which they would never sin.

In fact, back of the orthodox teaching on Original Sin is this very assumption, if one only thinks it through far enough. For the teaching is that if Adam had not sinned, then none of his descendants would have sinned. All that was necessary was for him to resist this one temptation he had, in order that he and all other human beings should inevitably resist all other temptations. Moreover, it is also the teaching of orthodox theologians that a few human beings have never actually sinned. This is said of the Blessed Virgin Mary and of John the Baptist. In His infinite knowledge of how human beings would react to their environment, God might have chosen either of these sinless human beings as the representative of the race instead of Adam. Why did not God choose either of them, and so prevent all human sin? Theology has no answer.

Nor is it really an answer to the problem to deny human freedom. Doubtless there would be no sin without free will, and in that sense no moral evil to explain. But there would still remain the acts which we call sins and we should have to reconcile them with God. Our nature—whether we are free or not—revolts against a brutal murder, a base betrayal. And how could an all-good God have deliberately planned them, made them necessary, as they would be on the supposition of determinism? We cannot answer. Determinism does not solve the problem of evil.

There is, then, no complete satisfactory rational solution to the problem of moral evil. Our puny finite minds find it difficult to reconcile sin with an all-good, an all-wise, and an all-powerful God. We bow in presence of the mystery.

I wish we could know the full answer. But search inspired and uninspired literature through and through, one will fail to find the complete solution. Considerations have been urged, answers have been given, accepted by some, rejected by others. And it is better frankly to admit that there is the problem, than to try to deceive ourselves and others by denying its existence.

But though a mystery with our present limited human outlook, it is far from involving such a fundamental contradiction as to demand the denial of theistic belief. We can still believe in God, and we can still believe in human freedom. We must cling to God, and to our own free-will as making us like to God. Amid the mystery and difficulty of the problem, we must cry out, "I believe, Lord, help my unbelief."

IV

The question of God's knowledge and power raises not only the problem of evil, which we have just considered, but also the problem of His providence as manifested in response to prayer. And this question of prayer in turn leads on to the problem of miracles in a scientific world. Professor Leuba, debating in the *Forum* magazine with Professor A. J. Thomson (September, 1927), maintained that such interference of God in the world through prayer or miracles was the essential point of conflict between religion and science.

Does God know of our prayers, and does He respond to them in any way? The considerations already suggested in regard to God's knowledge offer no particular difficulty to believing that God *knows* of our prayers. A *response* to prayer, however, raises two objections. One difficulty is the seeming implication of a change in God, and, therefore, of a certain imperfection. But since there is no past, present, and future for God, only an eternal now, we must not think of prayer as implying a change in God. Our praying and God's answer are both from God's standpoint outside of time and in His eternity. And though His response, assuming He really answers our prayer, takes place in time as far as we are concerned, it is not in time from God's side. It is part of His eternal activity.

This conception removes at least one difficulty some persons feel in accepting the possibility of God answering human prayers—the implication of a change in God. But it does not touch the difficulty most important for the modern mind— the introduction of the supernatural into the natural world. The modern mind, imbued with the scientific concept of a uniform nature, often balks at the idea of a spiritual power through prayer.

However, there are one or two considerations that make the approach to prayer more plausible even from the scientific standpoint. There are more things in heaven and earth than are dreamt of in Leuba's science as well as in Horatio's philosophy. We have hints of reservoirs of psychic power that cannot be completely explained or measured by science. There seems, at least at times for some individuals, such a thing as thought transference. The intense concentration of one person on another will apparently produce some impulse in the other that he attributes to a hunch, a presentiment. And if that is possible between human beings, may it not be possible also between God and His creatures? May not His response to prayer be some such action on the individual praying, or on the individual prayed for? Is this action by God really any more of a contradiction of science than the purely human psychic phenomena?

Moreover, in considering prayer we must distinguish between such response as I have just mentioned, and what would be miraculous. For instance, at the time that a friend would decide what train to take in making a visit to me, I may for some reason pray that he will take a train at a particular hour. If God responds to my prayer by transmitting it, as it were, to him, and allowing the intense desire on my part to be unknowingly communicated to my friend, there would not be anything miraculous about the matter. But if when I reach the station, hours after my friend must have taken the train, I pray that he should be on this particular train, I am really asking for a miracle. His decision cannot now be affected. If he took the train, then he is on it, and there is no use praying; whereas if he did not take the train, then to have him on it now would imply a miraculous transportation of him at incredible speed to put him there.

And while there would not necessarily be anything philosophically repugnant in the thought of such a miracle, for a sufficient reason, there does seem to be something rather puerile about expecting God to interfere in this way to save me from waiting half an hour in a railroad station until the next train comes in. It is on a par with the miracles of the apocryphal Gospels, and Christian feeling has always put them on an entirely different plane from the miracles of the canonical Scriptures.

There remains, nevertheless, the difficulty of reconciling a miracle for any reason with a scientific outlook on the universe. Is a miracle necessarily inconsistent with a reign of law? What becomes of uniformity if we allow the possibility of even one exception? And is it not true that many things which would have been looked upon as miraculous in the Middle Ages are now considered perfectly natural? Consequently, should we not rather take the view that either what is

[141]

called a miracle did not happen, or else that it was due to some natural power at present unexplained?

Well, I think we can approach the question best from the standpoint of what is perfectly natural, and yet which is an interference of some sort with the working out of a particular law. There is, for instance, the law of gravity. Yet every moment of the day individual men are preventing by acts of their free wills what would otherwise have happened by the operation of this law. When I hold a book in my hand, I am for the time being interfering with the force of gravity making that book fall to the floor. But nobody says that for this reason the law of gravity has been nullified, and the whole scientific world turned topsy-turvy. Another force has simply come into play, the power of my muscles flexed in a particular way. And the fact that my muscles are purely natural does not destroy this as an illustration of how the ordinary result of a natural force can be prevented without destroying science.

Suppose that the force of gravity had been interfered with in this regard by a supernatural power, instead of merely by my muscles. That would not essentially change the result from the standpoint of science—at least for libertarians.

Anyone who believes in human freedom ought to find no special difficulty in seeing that the structure of natural science does not collapse because a free act of some human will keeps a book from falling when otherwise it would fall. And while there are scientists who deny human freedom for precisely this reason, there are innumerable scientists just as eminent who find in it no difficulty.

How it is that a force above those at our command, and therefore above nature, or supernatural, can act in this world of ours is sometimes illustrated by the example of dimensions or powers. We live in a three-power, or three-dimension world. But we can conceive of a two-dimension world, and two-dimension living beings in that world. They would be confined within a plane, and a circle would be as much of a hindrance to locomotion as the Andes to us. Any manifestation in this two-dimension world of a three-dimension being—as for instance, stepping over a circle—would seem to the two-dimension beings just as much above their power, and therefore supernatural or miraculous, as the events transcending our powers seem miraculous to us.

But even though from time to time three-dimension beings did operate in a two-dimension world, that two-dimension world would still remain. There would be certain laws that would be natural for it. The scientists existing there would still have their science. And just as we can conceive of two-dimension beings as contrasted with the three-dimension beings we know, so we can conceive of the possibility of four dimensions, and five, and ten, and a hundred. We get finally to the infinite power of God. The manifestation of this Being with infinite powers in our three-dimension universe does not necessarily contradict the laws proper to that three-dimension world. Those laws remain.

And while it is true that the progress of science has shown that certain phenomena which previous ages considered supernatural are now known to be perfectly natural, yet that does not lead us to deny all possibility of the miraculous. Rather it should make us the more cautious in accepting the dogmatic statements of some scientists in regard to the possibility of miracles. For the corresponding dogmatic scientists of those earlier ages denied just as strenuously that these so-called miraculous events ever took place, because, they said, they are incompatible with science. If we admitted them, then we should have to discard science.

Today their confreres in science admit the events actually happened, but explain them naturally. And science has not been destroyed, as was predicted by the earlier scientists.

It is pure dogmatism to assume that miracles cannot happen. The really scientific attitude is to say that it all depends on the evidence in the case. If the alleged facts are well substantiated, then we should accept them. No preconceptions should stand in the way of giving the same credence to human testimony on this point as on any other.

And we are safe in saying that there are certain phenomena which cannot be natural, either because of special circumstances, or because of the power essentially involved. Science may show that sometimes there is apparent death, for instance, and that consequently what was called previously a miracle of coming back to life was in reality a recovery from merely apparent death. But science knows that sometimes death can be certainly established, and that if a person certainly dead lives again, it is because of a power above nature's forces.

There is nothing, then, in the nature of things to preclude the possibility of miracles and prayer. Such an interference by God in this physical world does not destroy science. The contention that modern science has ruled out prayer and miracles is based on a faulty analysis of science on the one hand, and of prayer and miracles on the other.

v

There is one other very interesting question of God's relation to His creatures, which should be considered, and that is: how did God bring this universe, and particularly human beings, into existence? Was it in the way described in the book of Genesis? Even though science does not go back of the beginning of things to their ultimate Cause, is it not brought into definite conflict with revealed religion on this point? For science is at present completely dedicated to an evolutionary attitude.

Well, the first thing that strikes the religious-minded person in trying to understand the Genesiac account of creation, is the fact that there are really two accounts in Genesis. The first account runs from the opening verse down to the fourth verse of the second chapter; and the second account begins there and continues for the rest of this second chapter. The accounts differ suffi-

[146]

ciently to make a reconciliation difficult. In the first account, for instance, we have the story divided into "days," and the order of creation implies that the earth was first covered with water before dry land appeared. In the second account, the earth seems to have been originally dry, and only later water was formed. According to the first account, God created man and woman apparently at the same time; in the second account we have the story of Eve's formation from a rib of Adam.

Because of these and other considerations, perfectly orthodox biblical students have long thought that the actual process of creation may have been in some evolutionary way. In fact, we get hints of such a view as far back as Gregory Nazianzen and Augustine of Hippo. They knew nothing, naturally, of modern scientific theories of evolution, and their theories would not be called scientific. But it is interesting to note that from a religious side they saw no difficulty in assuming that God endowed the first matter—whatever it was—with the powers necessary to develop into something else, without any direct and immediate interference on His part. There was no need, in their mind, because of the Genesiac account, to assume what has been called "special creation" for each new species.

And while there was a fierce conflict between scientists and theologians when scientists in the last century undertook to describe the process of evolution, that conflict has long ago died down in regard to the inanimate universe. Geologists or astronomers are very rarely called heretics today for their theories of cosmic evolution. And there are theologians who support, with restrictions, a theory of evolution, whether of plant or of animal life. Their chief concern seems to be to limit the dogmatic tendency of scientists to look upon evolution of animal forms as completely demonstrated. And considering the difficulties they made for themselves in the past by identifying the science of a particular day with religion or revelation, this attitude is only wise.

As might be supposed, the main problem agitating both scientists and theologians today is the question of man's evolution. And here it is necessary to understand clearly what is meant by "man." Is man simply an animal, differing only in degree from lower animals?

The theologian will not accept the concept of

man that makes him essentially the same as lower animals. From the theologian's standpoint, there must be superadded to man's material body an immaterial soul. And incidentally, the theologian has certain foremost scientists on his side in this contention. Notably Driesch, the biologist, finds man inexplicable on a purely mechanistic basis. And I suppose we are safe in saying that the tendency of scientists for the past ten or twenty years has been away from the idea that physics and chemistry can completely explain man.

It was a biologist of note, St. George Mivart, a contemporary of Charles Darwin, who first suggested that the theological position might be saved, and yet a scientific theory of evolution accepted, too, by making evolution apply to man's body alone. His book was called *The Genesis of Species,* and it still makes interesting reading.

According to this view, the Book of Genesis was not intended to teach an absolutely literal, scientific account of creation. All that it was intended to do was to insist on the fact of creation—not on the "how" of it. The "how" of creation may have been by God bringing into existence originally the elements of matter, whether as a primordial fire-mist or in some other form. Then by

THE NATURE OF GOD

laws which had been established for this primary material, it gradually developed, as the astronomers would hold, until there was formed the solar system of which our earth is a part. At first this earth was unfit for any living being. But in course of time, it changed to such an extent that life was called into existence, at first of a very elementary nature, and later as the environment changed, of a much more complex kind. Through æons of time—as many million years as scientists demand—life as we know it came to be.

At some point in the process, man emerged. That is, when by organic evolution a body capable of housing an essentially different soul—one possessing at least the rudiments of intelligence and freedom—had been prepared, it was inhabited by such a soul. And that was man. As far as the divine omnipotence is concerned, it would make no difference whether the human body was formed out of nothing, or out of dust, or out of animal ancestors. Any one of these processes would be in keeping with the Christian idea of the power and the wisdom and the dignity of God.

It is not repugnant to the absolute power of God that this emergence of man should have taken place more than once. There could have been so-called pre-Adamites. The theologians, how-ever, would affirm that as a matter of fact all human beings on earth today are descended from just one of these pairs of human beings.

And the tendency of modern anthropology is to agree with this theological view. A generation or two ago, it was quite common for some anthro-pologists to assert that the difference between various groups of men today demanded a multiple evolution. But now they are willing enough to admit that these differences can be accounted for in other ways, if enough time is allowed for the process. And if it is time the anthropologists want, theologians are ready to grant all the time the anthropologists ask. In short, the tendency of the anthropologists is away from tribal evolution and towards the theory of just one pair of original human beings.

I suppose that most good scientists would be willing to admit that science can never speak dog-matically on this particular question. There is no way now, and there seems no way in the future, for science to say definitely that all human beings are or are not descended from one original pair. And the finding of what are claimed as intermedi-ate remains does not really affect the theological position. If there was intelligence in these beings, then they were men. If they did not have intelligence, then they were not men.

Moreover, it should be borne in mind that "evolution" does not explain anything. How did different species originate? To say by "evolution" tells us nothing, practically. For "evolution," in such usage, is merely a name for our ignorance. We have to try to go back of that word, and explain evolution.

Darwin suggested that evolution came about by the multiplication of very minute changes, each change giving its possessors a little advantage in the struggle for existence, and so tending to be perpetuated. Modern biologists, however, look rather askance upon this particular feature of the theory. Acquired characteristics, they think, are not transmitted. And the differences due simply to the fact that no two individuals of a species are ever exactly alike, would tend to cancel out. That is, some differences would be favorable, others unfavorable. There would be no reason why the differences should all be in one direction—in the direction of producing more and more complicated organisms.

Consequently, the theory enjoying more favor

today among biologists considers that the changes took place rather suddenly, by what has been called "mutations." Perhaps the clearest illustration of something of the sort would be the development of birds from reptiles. If this change took place by very slow degrees, the first rudimentary wings would probably have been a hindrance rather than an advantage. The individuals thus afflicted would have been exterminated in the struggle for existence, instead of surviving. Whereas if there were a leap, a "saltation," the thing might have happened.

But "mutation" or "saltation" is also merely a word, like "evolution." That, too, needs explaining. Why do saltations occur? Nobody knows. It looks very much like the reintroduction of the idea of special creation. In fact, Dr. Austin H. Clark, biologist of the United States National Museum, in Washington, was reported recently as recognizing this fact (New York *Times*, January 21, 1929). "So far as regards the major groups of animals, the creationist seems to have the better of the argument," conceded Dr. Clark. "There is not the slightest evidence that any one of the major groups arose from any other. Each is a special animal, complex, related more or less closely to all the rest, and appearing, therefore, as a special creation."

Evolution offers no particular difficulty to the theist. It does not deserve all the noise that has been made about it. Much more fundamental are the problems which existed long before Darwin wrote his famous book on *The Origin of Species*. But the difficulty of believing in an all-good, an all-powerful, an all-knowing God who is so intimately present to each individual as almost to seem responsible for all human acts, is less than the difficulties involved in atheism. Not only does the theistic position give more dignity and comfort to humanity, it is also intellectually more defensible.

V. THE NATURE OF MAN

Human intelligence as essentially different from lower animals; difficulties of determinism; limitations of freedom; arguments for free will; difficulties of freedom.

V. THE NATURE OF MAN

I

THE essential difference between man and the lower animals, we have said, is that man possesses intelligence and freedom. But as the question of both freedom and intelligence is strenuously controverted, it will be well to spend some time on each of them.

The study of so-called animal intelligence has been confused and sterile, largely, and I wonder if this has not been because so many investigators have failed to define what they were looking for. What is intelligence? Sometimes intelligence has been described as the power of reasoning, or as the conscious using of means to an end. And these definitions, if properly understood, are good enough. But they must be interpreted as implying the use of abstract ideas. Abstraction is of the essence of intelligence. Without abstraction we do not have what can be called, strictly speaking, reasoning or intelligence in men.

We speak, for instance, of children reaching the

age of reason. Prior to that they have shown a much greater intelligence than any lower animal ever has, but we do not say that they have reasoning powers. They can use means to an end, such as getting a chair to reach a jam jar; they can associate sounds with objects and actions in a fairly elaborate language; and yet we realize an essential difference between their mental processes and those of an adult. The difference is in the power of abstraction. Young children associate concrete things, they do not abstract.

Ever since the theory of evolution became thoroughly established in scientific circles, an intensive study of the mental processes of lower animals has been carried on. The evolutionary theory in the opinion of a great many scientists implied that there was no essential difference between man and lower animals, but only a difference of degree. Consequently, some lower animals should exhibit at least the rudiments of intelligence.

The first stage of this study consisted in the collection of more or less authentic stories of animals supposedly illustrating a power of thinking. Elephants were alleged to carry tree trunks quite a distance, pile them on top of one another, and so climb to some height that otherwise they could not reach. Monkeys were reported to realize they could not cross a stream at a certain point, then make a sort of reconnaissance until they found a spot where the stream was narrow enough to cross. And of course domesticated animals came in for their share of such stories.

Then came a period when scientists attempted to study the intelligence of animals by some sort of laboratory method. Particular animals were selected, and the tests carefully devised. One experiment, for instance, was shutting a dog up in a cage with a contrivance that he could operate with his nose, if only he found it out, and timing his escapes. The fact that the dog increased his speed in escaping was said to show that he connected the latch with opening the door, and was really thinking how he could get out. He was using a means to an end.

In all such stories or experiments, however, there need be no more than the association of visual images. And that does not necessarily imply real thinking. When in experiment a bunch of bananas is suspended beyond the ordinary reach of a monkey, but a box is put in another corner of the cage, it is not a strictly scientific conclusion to say that the monkey is thinking because he moves the box over to the side of the bananas, mounts upon it, and gets the fruit. The association of the picture of the height of the bananas, his own height, and his height on the box, will be sufficient to account for the result.

As a matter of fact, those scientists who have relied upon such incidents to prove the intelligence of animals, have themselves not thought through the question sufficiently. They did not define their own problem in such a way as to exclude all extraneous matter. And as a result, they allowed an association of images to obtrude itself into the answer. They should have defined thinking more carefully. And when so defined, thinking implies the formation of abstract ideas.

Because this is so, other scientists attempted to find at least some animals who did show an ability to use abstract ideas or symbols. The most famous case, probably, was the German horse. This animal was supposed to count up to a certain number, to add, and to subtract, by giving with his forefoot the proper number of taps. In *The Literary Digest* for November 17, 1928, is an account of a pony that was even more extraordinary. It is not told by a scientist, but it is along the same lines as recognized scientists have described. "Mr.

THE NATURE OF MAN

Barrett," so the story goes, "handed me a slate and I wrote down, one under the other, the numbers 2,234, 5,716, and 7,934. To make the addition more difficult, Mr. Barrett added 4,283 and 7,765. I held the slate before the pony, who shook his head vigorously, and at Mr. Barrett's question announced he could give the result. From his racks he took down the figures to make the total 27,932, which is correct. In the same way he divided 456 by five, and did other sums."

A number of other similar cases have been examined, and it has always been shown that there is some communication between the animal and a human being. Sometimes this communication may be unconscious. In the case of the German horse, apparently, the professor did not realize himself that he was showing by his eye the correct answer to the mathematical questions, and that the horse would stop tapping with his foot when he saw a certain expression in his master's eye. But when he could not see his master, he could not do his sums.

Joseph Dunninger, for instance, a professional magician and mind-reader of the Houdini school, asserts that "animals never possess what is called human intelligence. They have fine memories, and can be taught intricate, difficult things. But at best they are only actors, in the sense that they simply memorize certain movements and actions, and do them as told. They do not and cannot think, read, or write. At least I never knew of one that could. Nor do I know of any person who ever saw such an animal."

Dunninger then gives the story of what a fox terrier trained by him could do, and it is even more remarkable than the pony's achievements. But he explains how the whole thing was done. It was merely a matter of training, and the devising of an apparatus that seemed to preclude interference on his part. During the performance, Dunninger would be in another room out of sight of the dog. Nevertheless he was communicating with the dog by a very clever contrivance. The dog did what he was signaled to do.

All the stories of the language of animals can also be reduced to a matter of associating images, or of associating sounds with images. It is all as simple, really, as dog Tray associating that sound "Tray" with himself. He gets to know that this means him. But just as men called dogs by names for thousands of years without for this reason attributing intelligence to the dogs, so today the fact that animals associate certain sounds with fear, or with food, or with danger does not mean intelligence.

But there is one consideration in this regard that seems to be quite conclusive. If animals could think, and could transmit their thought to other animals, would there not be some rudiments of an animal language, and would there not be the gradual increase of knowledge among animals. But all the illustrations given of animal language can be accounted for on the basis of association of sounds with images. None of them show the use of sounds as symbols, in the way that human beings use sounds. There is no abstraction. All sounds for animals mean certain concrete things, such as milk, feeding time, etc. They never mean such abstract conceptions as beauty, justice, truthfulness.

And there is no evidence that animals have increased their store of knowledge. If they really thought, reasoned things out, found that certain ways of doing things were better than others, and could communicate this by language to their fellow animals there would certainly in all these centuries of their existence be some evidence of an increase in knowledge. But birds are still building their nests as their remote ancestors built them, dogs are still acting on the same instincts.

So far no conclusive proof of animal intelligence has ever been offered. And those scientists who maintain that animals must have intelligence, because there cannot be any such essential difference between men and lower animals, are really adopting just as aprioristic an attitude as any theologian. In fact, it is worse than assumption. It is flying in the face of whatever evidence we have. For all the evidence points in the direction of such an essential difference, to the fact that men have intelligence and lower animals do not have intelligence.

II

The second essential difference between men and lower animals is that men possess free will. Curiously enough, extreme evolutionists take a very different attitude towards human and animal freedom from that which they take towards human and animal intelligence. As regards intelligence, their object is to show that both men and lower animals have intelligence; whereas as regards free will, their object is to show that neither men nor lower animals are free. Our purpose, therefore, is accomplished if we can show that men do have freedom, as there is no question of lower animals having free will.

To avoid confusion, we ought to start with a definition of freedom, for we have seen what confusion has been introduced into the discussion of animal intelligence by using the term vaguely. But free will is not an easy thing to define. Perhaps the best way to go about explaining the idea of free will is from the standpoint of determinism. According to determinism, everything in this world, including all the acts of human beings, is absolutely determined by fixed mechanical laws. Everything is necessitated. Nothing could possibly have been different. Whereas according to the libertarians, some acts of human beings are not determined. They might have been different. The number of these freely willed acts is probably much less than the popular estimate, but it is sufficient for the libertarian view that there should be at least some.

Certainly there are difficulties connected with free will or with indeterminism. But just as we began a consideration of God's existence by taking up certain difficulties inherent in a denial of His existence, so it will be best to begin our considera-

ties inherent in determinism. All the difficulties
tion of indeterminism by taking up some difficul-
are not by any means on the side of free will.
There is a fine crop of difficulties to be solved by
anyone who clings to the deterministic attitude.
First of all, determinism would destroy all
moral values. There would be no moral difference between killing a fly and deliberately running over a child playing in the street. There
would be no moral difference between death coming from a lightning bolt, and death coming from
electrocution inflicted by a human enemy. All
these acts would be equally determined, equally
the result of blind mechanical laws. The human
being driving the car running over the child would
be as much a machine as the automobile itself.
The driver would no more be master of his own
acts than the machine is master of its acts.

And as the real worth of personality depends on
the power of the human being to direct his own
acts, there could be no value to personality. It
would be as absurd to talk of the personality of
Lindbergh as to talk of the personality of his air-
plane. Both of them would be machines, and
merely machines. Lindbergh would deserve no
more credit for his feat than does his machine.

He simply could not have done otherwise. It would have been impossible for him to lose his nerve, to make a mistake in reckoning, to become discouraged and turn back.

Moreover, determinism by making the greatest crimes inevitable would lead to pessimism. William James has worked this out very effectively in his essay on the freedom of the will, published in his volume called *The Will to Believe*. I can give only a bare outline here of James' development of this thought, and to be appreciated the argument ought to be read in its entirety.

James instances what was at that time a famous murder, the Brockton affair. To bring the illustration down to date we could speak of the Snyder case or of the Hickman murder. Now on the theory of determinism, everything in the universe demanded just such incidents. Nothing else would fit into the total scheme of things. We may think that such acts were shocking, but the determinist maintains that they were as inevitable as sunrise. The whole of modern science, the whole sidereal universe would collapse on the supposition of anything else being even possible. But as we cannot help calling such acts bad, we are in the position of saying that what must inevitably have been performed by human beings is bad, and demanded by the whole universe.

However, if a universe demands bad acts, how about the universe itself? Is not the universe bad? And if the universe is inevitably bad, do we not have a pronounced pessimism?

Moreover, the difficulty of the determinist position in this connection is not yet exhausted. The reaction of disgust which normal human beings feel at such crimes as Hickman committed is also determined. Our same universe which determines certain individuals to commit these horrible murders, also determines everyone else to be shocked at them. So that we have part of a deterministic universe determined to do what is going to be looked upon by the rest of the universe as a misfit, as something which had better not have been.

Is there not thus introduced into the universe an insoluble contradiction? For if the murders in question are really determined by the universe, and so could not have been otherwise, are they not in harmony with the universe? And being in harmony with the universe, should not all parts of the universe—other human beings included—realize that harmony? Should they not be determined to recognize the fitness of all these acts, because they fit and nothing else can fit? How can a deterministic universe determine any part of itself to recognize disharmony in what is determined?

Again, determinism leads not only to a denial of free will but to a denial of the validity of all reasoning. As has been pointed out, if all my acts are determined, then my reaction to the arguments for or against freedom is also determined. Reasoning becomes as mechanistic as volition. And consequently there is no discrimination possible between arguments. Reasoning loses all meaning.

Burnett Hillman Streeter has put this very clearly in his book called *Reality:* "If the Determinist is right in denying the existence of spontaneous initiative," he writes, "the application of his principle cannot be limited to action; his argument, if it proves anything, proves that wishes and thoughts, quite as much as deeds, are mechanically determined. The Freudians so far are right in emphasizing this. But here comes the difficulty: if Determinism is a sound theory, then it is determined which arguments shall appeal to me as valid and which shall appear to be fallacies. It follows, then, that my thinking the case for Determinism conclusive constitutes no reason at all for believing it to be so; I think so merely because some purely accidental circumstances of heredity and environment have determined that I should be the kind of person to whom the arguments for Determinism appeal. And if my opponent is convinced by the arguments for Free Will, that is not because the arguments *are* superior, but merely because, by his heredity and environment, it is determined that he shall think them so. Accordingly, if the Determinist is right, reasoning can prove nothing; it is merely an ingenious method for providing us with apparently rational excuses for believing what in any case we cannot help believing. But if all reasoning is a 'pathetic fallacy,' then the reasons for believing in Determinism itself are fallacious. Not only that; unless reason is that which can *discriminate*, there is no criterion of truth and falsehood; all knowledge collapses; one hypothesis is as good as another, and Science itself is a fairy tale. This conclusion can be avoided only if we see that as a necessary postulate of reasoning, there must be inherent in the nature of thought enough of spontaneity to enable it to discriminate between true and false; and that means, in its reaction to material submitted to it, to *choose* between two or more alternatives. Were thought no more than an automatic reflex action of the organism to circumstances, the nature of that reaction would be predetermined; the mind might react by judging statements to be either true or false, but such judgment would be determined, not by the actual merit of the case, but merely by the exact nature of the stimulus, emotional or otherwise, given by the way the statement was put. True, our judgments often do come very near to being of this nature; but the essential difference between prejudice and real knowledge consists in our having *some* capacity to rise above such automatic reactions" (Macmillan, 1926, pp. 75, 76).

III

There is one other consideration with regard to determinism that ought to have a special appeal to those familiar with scientific methods. From a scientific standpoint, the test of a theory is always its application to the world of fact. Does the theory work? Or does it break down when tested?

After all, reality is the great criterion by which any theory, whether philosophical or scientific, must be judged. And for a theory such as determinism, the test is life itself. We should ask ourselves, Is determinism livable? Can it be consistently applied to the conditions of everyday life? Can one live as a determinist?

Any theory which is impossible of application, is by that very fact convicted of falsehood. The universe has to fit together, if we are to have any such thing as knowledge, science, reasoning. If one opposes this view, and asserts that a theory does not have to fit life, he is certainly not taking this position on scientific grounds.

What, then, do we find when we try to apply the theory of determinism to life? Man does not live by bread alone, but assuredly he does not live by any such word as determinism. When we begin observing the conduct of others, we never find a consistent determinist. I suppose that no professor of determinism in class ever applied his theory to the conduct of his pupils. If a student went to a night club instead of preparing a paper, the professor never accepted as an excuse that the student could not help doing this because of his heredity, environment, and previous manner of acting. The professor talked and acted as if the student might have written the paper. The professor of determinism held the student responsible for his conduct.

Of course, if the professor were taken to task for inconsistency, he could reply that he punished the student with a full realization that the act had been determined. But the student had been determined in this particular way because his reaction lacked the stimulus that would have come from the memory of a punishment previously administered for a similar lapse. Consequently, the professor was simply introducing the element of punishment now so that it would determine future reactions.

But who can doubt that such an answer is merely a rationalization of an instinctive reaction on the professor's part? As a matter of fact, he talks and acts as if other people had a responsibility for their conduct. And if a particular professor denies that he so acts, he cannot deny that many other persons so act. He cannot deny that many persons not only act as if others were free, but that they believe others to be free. We have, then, the fundamental inconsistency of individuals being determined to think that others are freely responsible. This is surely a topsy-turvy world if a deterministic universe determines certain parts of it to think that they are free when they are determined.

[173]

W. H. Mallock in his book, *The Reconstruction of Religious Belief,* has worked out with extraordinary persuasiveness the inconsistency of the determinists. No professor of determinism, he suggests, in saying good-by to his fiancée when she is going on a journey, would address her in deterministic language: "Considering the physical brain cells you have inherited, and the sharpness of the sensitive images I have impressed upon them, I am confident that you will retain such an attractive picture of myself that no other man will be able to replace me in your affections." The professor, like every other man, in spite of his protestations of determinism, talks in such circumstances as if his fiancée had some power within herself of governing her actions. If the professor talked like a determinist, his fiancée would probably be "determined" not to marry him, and he would be compelled—if not determined—to pass his life in single blessedness.

But if the determinist professor has somehow carried through his intention of marrying this woman, and afterwards she proves unfaithful to her marriage vows, still less does he say calmly to himself that she could not possibly have done otherwise. He does not carry through his deter-

[174]

ministic attitude, and say: "Unfortunately the sensitive images I impressed upon her brain cells were too weak to resist the images of another man. She was like a photographic plate exposed briefly to a light lacking actinic rays, and later exposed properly to a stronger light. The second image had to obliterate the first." On the contrary, the professor, in spite of his brave determinism, holds his wife just as responsible for infidelity as if he had been a professor of indeterminism. His theory of determinism breaks down in the face of the hard facts of life.

Herbert Spencer was a determinist. Yet he was at great pains to show that he, rather than Darwin, was the first to conceive and formulate the general theory of evolution. But on the theory of determinism Spencer deserved no credit for ante-dating Darwin. Moreover, to emphasize the inconsistency, Spencer spent his later years, as Mallock points out, in compiling "two enormous volumes devoted entirely to a microscopic biography of himself—to the difficulties and discouragements he encountered and his own strength of will in overcoming them. Spencer's life was, no doubt, one of singular intellectual heroism, and he cannot be blamed if he was modestly conscious of the fact;

[175]

but the admiration which the world feels for him, and the claims made by him for himself, are intelligible only on the supposition that he possessed a free-will of his own, which, while dismissing it in theory as a village gossip's illusion, he, like everybody else, accepted in practice as a reality. Thus one of the few deterministic thinkers who have deliberately attempted to interpret concrete life by determinism is in his own person one of the most interesting witnesses to the impossibility of interpreting it intelligibly without a covert reintroduction of the plain man's belief in freedom" (*Reconstruction of Religious Belief*, Harper's, 1905, p. 87).

There is, however, not only this practical inconsistency among the determinists. Not only do they act as if there were free will, they actually when expounding *ex professo* the theory of determinism use language which implies freedom. The late Professor E. C. Hayes, of the University of Illinois, can be selected as an illustration, because he gives us such a clear example of this. He is a frank determinist, and states the determinist position in the orthodox way. "One factor in the causation of our course of action," he writes, "is found in external conditions; another is heredity;

and a third proximate cause is habit, judgment, principle—the stored results of our past experience and reflection. The activity of each hour is the resultant that issues from the meeting of these three: hereditary capacity, the effects of past activity and experience, and external occasion" (*Sociology and Ethics*, Appleton, 1921, p. 59).

But when Professor Hayes goes on to analyze human conduct more in detail, he uses language that might be put into the mouth of a libertarian. In fact, he actually employs the word "freedom." "What then," he asks, "does the word freedom mean to the determinist? It means *power to achieve ends approved by our own intelligence*" (p. 60). "According to the natural science view, our freedom, negatively considered, is freedom from external control, not the absence of external factors in the causation of conduct but the preponderance of internal factors, the power to resist those solicitations of the passing occasion which are inconsistent with our own established judgments and sentiments. Positively considered, it is the power to execute a definite policy and purpose" (p. 62).

If language means anything, then Hayes has given away the determinist position. His power

to attain ends intellectually approved certainly re-
introduces the element of self-determination demanded by the libertarians. Hayes asks what the
word "freedom" means to a determinist. One
would think that "freedom" would mean a denial
of determinism, that freedom and determinism
are mutually exclusive. But the writer wants to
eat his cake and keep it. He wants both freedom
and determinism.

Professor C. Judson Herrick, of the University
of Chicago, is another determinist. But when he
came to write a book called *Fatalism or Freedom*,
he, too, used the word "freedom." "We do have
the power," he writes, "by intelligent choices so
to direct our conduct that we place ourselves in
receptive attitudes towards the sources of mental
strength just as we can decide whether to eat and
nourish our bodies or to diet and reduce our
weight" (p. 65). And in the next paragraph, he
speaks of "this power to choose, that is, to shape
our conduct in view of one out of several possible
future contingencies."

After reading such language as Hayes and Herrick use, one wonders if the controversy between
determinists and indeterminists is not one of words,
rather than of realities. For the determinists

seem to be fighting a "causeless" freedom that the best libertarian philosophers never advocated, and at the same time they seem to mean about the same thing by their determinism that the more moderate libertarians mean by indeterminism. How far determinists and libertarians are really in agreement will be clearer after discussing the positive arguments for freedom. and the limitations of freedom.

IV

We have just considered certain serious objections against the theory of determinism. But the rejection of determinism does not imply acceptance of the view that all acts of human beings are free. No libertarian ever held the fantastic theory that all acts of a man were free, and it would be a caricature of free will to represent it in this way. Libertarians may differ as to the freedom of particular acts, or as to what proportion of acts is probably free, but all libertarians admit that freedom is very seriously limited.

In discussing determinism we contented ourselves with describing freedom by contrast with determinism. But as it is a false notion of freedom which leads some to determinism, it will be well now to define freedom more accurately.

Freedom of the will is the power of choosing between various possible courses of action. Freedom is not causeless volition, nor is it motiveless willing. Whenever an act is free, there must always be more than one motive, and the will chooses between these motives. The will is its own cause. We can, indeed, take over Professor Hayes' definition of freedom as "the power to achieve ends intellectually approved." What is meant by this power of freedom will appear more clearly if we consider certain limitations placed upon it. There is, of course, the limitation arising from environment. Each one of us has a special social inheritance limiting our freedom of action in many directions. For one brought up in the United States it is practically impossible to become a Tibetan monk. And, contrariwise, for a Tibetan monk to become a Christian is also practically impossible. Free will does not mean the ability to do anything, no matter how contradictory that may be to our previous ways of acting and manner of thought.

Much less does freedom of the will mean ability to overcome all physical conditions. The mere willing to be well will not cure tuberculosis. The reaction of mind on body may be important in its influence, but the will is nevertheless circumscribed and limited by the physical. It was long ago said in Scripture that man cannot by taking thought add one cubit to his stature. Nor can he by a mere fiat affect material objects external to himself and change lead into gold. Free will, in the view of sensible libertarians, is not, as Hayes implied, a magical or mystical power.

Freedom of the will does not mean freedom from external restraint, as we say a person is free as contrasted with a prisoner. It does not mean the power to disregard completely all social environment. Freedom of the will means only the power of choosing sometimes between two courses of action, both of which are presented to the will as desirable.

But not only does social inheritance limit freedom. Physical inheritance also limits it. There may be a predisposition in one direction or another because of one's inherited physical constitution. For instance, the inherited nervous system of a particular individual may be such as to demand a certain stimulation that can be obtained through alcohol. The man with such a body is less free than the man who has no such demand made upon him, and his freedom may even be completely destroyed in this one direction, though he remains free in other regards.

Or a child can be affected by shocks to its nervous system during the pregnancy of its mother. This is not the old idea that children could be marred in various ways by what the mother thought, but the perfectly reasonable position that the child while it is part of its mother, depending on her for nourishment, may be vitally affected by what affects the mother.

Still more can the will-power of an individual be affected by his psycho-physical constitution. There are many diseases which can reduce responsibility. A person suffering acutely from neurasthenia may be practically powerless to resist moods of depression, and in some such mood may even take his own life. Epilepsy, too, while the spell is on one, more completely than neurasthenia destroys the freedom of the will. And there are various neuroses and psychoses limiting freedom in one way or another.

Moreover, chronic diseases sometimes affect the disposition. A person may be irritable, sensitive, given to fits of anger because of the physical constitution. It is the fashion among some psychologists today to attribute everything to the ductless glands. Very possibly these glands do affect personality in some way. There is nothing in this that would be inconsistent with the doctrine of free will. It has long been recognized, for instance, that the secretions of the glands connected with the reproductive organs may cause very strong desires for sensual satisfaction. Whether a person has a cold or a passionate disposition will be determined largely by the secretions of these glands. And it may even happen that in a particular individual these glands are in such an abnormal condition as to destroy complete responsibility. Some responsibility is left, but it is not the complete responsibility of normal individuals. And if this is true of the glands connected with reproduction, it may be true of other glands, too, with a consequent elimination of the possibility of some acts being free, or completely free, in some individuals.

There may be a physical condition, glandular or otherwise, back of some abnormal cravings manifested in certain individuals. These cravings may be erotic, or they may have to do with something entirely different. The Freudians undoubtedly err in reducing everything to sex. I see no reason why the abnormal craving of some people for drugs of one sort or another should be con-

sidered a phase of sex, nor do I see why the existence of such cravings in some should completely
prove the impossibility of all freedom whatever
in anyone.

Closely connected with many of the above considerations that lessen the force of free will, is
the question of habit. We are so constituted that
sometimes a customary way of reacting to certain
stimuli becomes so strong as to make refusal so to
react impossible. The individual's freedom in this
regard has been destroyed. Sometimes this is in
regard to cocaine, morphine, alcohol, tobacco.
Sometimes it is in regard to words or expressions.
A perfectly obvious habit of this sort, condition-
ing freedom, is linguistic accent. Because I grew
up to maturity in the United States, I shall never
be able to speak French like a native. My vocal
habits of pronunciation acquired through years of
English are too strong.

Besides the limitations I have already mentioned
in regard to freedom we have certain psychological
compulsions. At times these compulsions are
clearly recognizable as such, and proceed even as
far as a neurosis of some sort. Again they may
require the delicate analysis of a professional
psychologist to unearth and bring to light. Some

of these compulsions can be overcome, and not infrequently the mere recognition of the mechanism by which one's conduct has been determined in the past is sufficient to break the spell. But at other times the compulsions persist for life, and it is impossible to conquer them. While the compulsion lasts, there may be no freedom in regard to the object of the compulsion.

Akin to these compulsions are suggestions from without. Undoubtedly some people can be played upon by the skilful through suggestion, without realizing that the impulse is given to them and that they are not acting freely. The most extreme example of such suggestion is the abnormal condition of hypnotic sleep. While in that condition the subject has really surrendered his will, at least to a large extent, into the keeping of someone else. He has become an automaton. He can help the first hypnotization, but once in that somnambulistic state, he cannot—within limits— resist the suggestions made to him by the hypnotizer.

What is an even greater encroachment upon freedom, the subject sometimes cannot help carrying out in his waking moments what was suggested during the hypnotic sleep. The hypnotizer foreseeing the conditions that will arise after the awakening, can suggest a certain reaction, and the subject carries that out without realizing that he is not free.

This particular phenomenon of hypnotism is another complicating element in this very complicated question of free will. For one of the strongest arguments for the possession of free will, as I have insisted, is the consciousness of such freedom. It is hard to see how consciousness could bear any clearer testimony to freedom than it does. And it is hard to see how consciousness could bear false testimony in this regard. But on the other hand, we have the same testimony of consciousness in a person who has been hypnotized, awakened, but is still subject to a suggestion given during hypnotic sleep. As far as that person's consciousness goes, he thinks that he is acting just as freely as if he had never been hypnotized. Yet it is certain that he is not free. He cannot help following the suggestion, although he is not now conscious of the suggestion.

As we have seen, for nearly every argument against freedom, there is a very satisfactory objection to show that the deterministic argument cannot be sound. But on the other hand, the determinists will of course advance an objection against every argument in favor of freedom, attempting to show that the free will argument cannot be sound. The question of course presents difficulties but there is a way of solving it on even purely rational grounds. And I suppose that ultimately some may come to accept the doctrine of freedom, much as Ruskin did. He tells us that when quite a small child he jumped up one step or two steps, varying from one to the other, and decided that he was the one who determined for himself whether it would be one step or two. His belief in his own freedom was never shaken. Though he did give up almost all orthodox Christian faith, he never gave up his belief in free will.

The weight of argument is for the freedom of the will. And from a practical standpoint, one can face life consistently on the basis of freedom, whereas no determinist has ever been consistent. I "choose" to be a libertarian, and in so choosing I do not think that I am determined. But if this choice of mine offends my determinist friends, they can only pity me, and continue to muddle their brains over the problem of how a determinist universe produced libertarians.

[187]

V

The survey we have just made of determinism shows that there are numerous difficulties for those who deny freedom. There are difficulties, it is true, connected with indeterminism, and we shall consider them frankly later on, but assuredly the difficulties are not all on the side of free will. A scientist does not avoid all intellectual problems by falling back on determinism. In fact, from some standpoints, he seems to be undermining his own science. And all in all, I should say that the difficulties of the determinist are considerably greater than the difficulties of the libertarian. Yet it seems to be chiefly the difficulties of free will that make certain minds accept the alternative of determinism. And because of this mental attitude on the part of so many, we began with the difficulties those ought to face who deny freedom. The difficulties of determinism ought almost of themselves to make one accept indeterminism as the lesser intellectual evil.

But the difficulties of determinism are not the only arguments that can be brought forward in support of free will. Such difficulties can be looked upon as negative arguments, and there are in addition some very positive arguments in favor of liberty.

First among the arguments for free will is the fact of a consciousness of freedom. We are as certain of feeling free as we can be of anything. And ultimately we must depend upon consciousness for all knowledge. Consciousness is the most intimate knowledge we possess, and indeed the only direct knowledge. Idealists can argue with some plausibility that no objective world exists, that what practical people call an objective world exists only in the conceiving mind. And even practical people must admit that knowledge coming from the senses is an interpretation of effects produced indirectly, rather than direct apprehension. When, for instance, I say that I "see" a dog, what I really mean is that I am conscious of a certain sensation through the optic nerve, and that I interpret this sensation as reporting an objective dog.

Consciousness, then, is the ultimate basis of all knowledge. And if the testimony of consciousness is to be ruled out in regard to freedom, it can only be on the ground of the most certain proof that we are deceived. The mere assertion that consciousness is deceived in registering freedom, or that freedom is incompatible with a world of science, will not be sufficient ground for denying freedom. For if we are to throw consciousness overboard in a field where consciousness can have direct knowledge, then we must discard consciousness in those fields where its knowledge is at best indirect. All reasoning, all science, become impossible. There is nothing left except an out and out skepticism. We must doubt the testimony of consciousness even to our own existence.

If we know anything at all, surely we know our own freedom. Consciousness could not be clearer on any point than it is on the point of our being able to choose between various courses of action. And, in fact, determinists themselves use this very word "choose." They cannot get away from some expression of this idea of freedom. Assuming that the testimony of consciousness is valid for anything, then it is valid for the possession of freedom.

But let us develop a little the ways in which consciousness testifies to freedom. We have the question of deliberation and decision. We have presented to us several different courses of action. There is, for instance, the question of a divorced man confronted with the question of marrying a second time during the life of his first wife. He deliberates over the problem. All his natural impulses lead to marriage. But he does not rush into it. He weighs the question pro and con. He marshals reasons for and against. His decision comes only after a long period of reflection.

Is he determined to one course rather than another? Well, as far as his consciousness goes, it tells him that he freely chooses. And sometimes at least, the choice will be against the natural impulses, against what would seem to be the course that would be determined. He conquers his desires because his intellect tells him anything else would be wrong. There is finally decision.

And this happens constantly in matters that have no particular moral bearing. It may be the purchase of a necktie, or the taking of a journey. It may be to read one book rather than another. In every field of human activity men are conscious of these free choices. If we are really determined in all these matters, it is hard to see why consciousness lies to us in this way. It could not tell us any more clearly that we are free, if we were really free.

On the other hand, consciousness does not always bear this testimony to freedom. Sometimes we know that desire proves too strong for the will.

We regret our weakness in yielding, but we realize clearly enough that we could not help it. The impulse of the moment pushed us over the edge without that freedom to which consciousness testifies on other occasions.

For instance, there is the familiar reflex action. A fly lights upon our nose, and we instinctively brush it away. There was no freedom in the act, and consciousness does not tell us that there was freedom. Or a man insults us, and immediately there is a hot retort, or even a blow struck. The action was not free.

Now on deterministic principles, it is impossible to explain how—assuming all actions are determined—consciousness reports that some actions are determined, but that other actions are free. Surely the testimony of consciousness ought to be determined always in one direction. It would be hard enough to reconcile the testimony of consciousness of freedom with determinism, if consciousness always reported in one way. It is doubly hard to reconcile determinism with varying reports of consciousness, sometimes that we are free, sometimes that we are determined. Life becomes a mere jumble instead of being the orderly process demanded by science.

This distinction between the testimony of consciousness on various occasions is brought out even more clearly in regard to remorse and repentance than in regard to deliberative decision. There are some actions about which we feel remorse, in the sense that we not only regret them, but we feel a certain shame at having done them. And in the shame there is included the idea that we might have done otherwise. This is an essential element for remorse. It is the element distinguishing remorse from mere regret.

For instance, a young man may feel regret that he could not send his invalid mother to an expensive sanatorium. But if he simply could not do it because he did not have the money, there is no remorse. On the other hand, if he had the money, and refused to send her because he wanted to spend the money on himself, then when her eyes were closed in death there might be remorse.

The very familiar feeling of remorse is but another witness of consciousness to the possession of freedom. And there is no way, on deterministic grounds, for explaining how consciousness distinguishes between regret and remorse. If we are never free, and therefore there should only be regret, how is it that consciousness is determined to register a quite different feeling—remorse? It is a hopeless mystery on the assumption of determinism.

Moreover, we sometimes feel a sense of moral obligation to act in a particular way. All one's social inheritance, all one's self-interest seems to lead in another direction. And yet there is the sense that one ought to act otherwise. Without freedom there can be no moral "ought." The word has no meaning on the assumption of determinism. "Ought" implies freedom.

An illustration of such a sense of obligation, running counter apparently to everything that might be expected to be determined, is the question of religious conversion. A young girl raised in an atmosphere of New England puritanism, breathing in a hatred of Catholicism based on the deepest prejudice, comes to feel an obligation to join the Catholic Church. All her self-interest leads in the direction of repressing any such impulse. But she feels the moral obligation to follow the impulse.

But consciousness, besides bearing direct testimony to freedom, is in another way, too, an argument for free will. For if everything is determined, how does it come about that we are deter-

THE NATURE OF MAN

mined to feel a consciousness of freedom? If the
world is not a crazy house, ought we not, on deterministic principles, be compelled to feel that we
are determined—assuming that we really are determined? Otherwise, there is introduced into
the universe an insoluble contradiction. One of
the elements in a deterministic world is giving testimony at variance with the actual facts. We
might rather say, paradoxically, that on deterministic principles themselves, since we feel a consciousness of freedom—and therefore would be
determined so to feel—we must be free.

Moreover, on the assumption of determinism,
as we have indicated previously, there could be no
moral quality to any acts, and hence no real moral
obligation. And it is appalling to consider what
would be the condition of the world if the moral
sense were completely destroyed. Society is bad
enough now, when men have a sense of moral
obligation and disregard it. But society would be
a hundred times worse if there were no such restraining influence whatever. It would be each
man for himself with a vengeance, and devil take
the hindmost.

Finally there is the metaphysical argument from
the conception of infinite good. Metaphysics is

somewhat out of fashion in our time and generation, but it nevertheless affords a sound argument.
What is it that leads the will to act in a particular
way? It is the conception of good. The will can
balance one good against another. If the intellect
could conceive of only one course as being good, or
leading to the possession of a good, the will would
have to take that course. The will would be
determined. But the intellect can always conceive
of a good greater than the one immediately presented to it. For the will can have presented to it
the conception of infinite good. And consequently
the will is not always determined to any particular
finite good.

VI

We have just seen that there are some very solid
arguments in favor of freedom. But we must
admit, on the other hand, that there are very serious difficulties connected with free will. One of
the most fundamental of these difficulties is somewhat similar to the difficulty faced by the determinists—that when one analyzes the nature of
freedom far enough, one seems to be implying determinism. A good libertarian, of course, repudi-
ates the idea of causeless volition. He says that
the will does not act without motive, but merely

chooses between various motives. It is unfair, therefore, to represent freedom as meaning action without any motive.

All this is true enough. But if the query be pushed farther than this, and the question asked: Why, then, does the will choose one motive rather than another? the only answer that can be given is because the will itself makes one motive stronger than another. And what is the cause of the will making one motive stronger than another? It must be either the motive itself or the will itself. If it is the motive itself, then the will could not have acted otherwise, it was determined. But if it was the will making one motive stronger than another, then in reality the will acts without motive in doing this. We have motiveless or causeless volition. The will is its own cause.

Dr. James H. Ryan is a confirmed libertarian. I quote from him because he has faced this difficulty more squarely than anyone else I know, and his answer seems to me to bring out more effectively the sort of ultimate impasse against which one comes up. "Freedom," he writes in his *Introduction to Philosophy*, "is not motiveless willing. No rational action is possible unless it is inspired by a motive. The free-willist, however,

[197]

denies that this motive must be confused with something either in man's environment or his character. Motives are presented to reason, and reason chooses *not without* but *between* motives. If only one motive should be presented, the consequent act would not be free.

"Neither do we deny that man, in his choices, follows the 'strongest motive.' The very fact that he acts on a motive makes the particular motive, as far as the individual goes, the strongest. . . . Granted that he always acts according to the strongest motive, what is it that makes a particular motive the strongest? If it is not man's character, nor the mechanical laws of nature, but his inherent power to determine for himself the strength of motives, then such an objection proves nothing at all against the doctrine of freedom of the will" (Macmillan, 1924; p. 255).

But the act of the will in electing to follow one motive rather than another must be accounted for just like any other act of the will. It is granted that the will does not act without a motive. What motive, then, makes the will follow one of the two or more motives presented to it above the other motive, or other motives?

We are confronted by another of those seeming

antinomies which the finite mind not infrequently meets in its analysis of the phenomena presented to it by this universe of ours. We find similar seeming contradictions on all sides of us. Extended particles of matter, for instance, must theoretically be divisible. But if they are divisible, must not one get ultimately to what is not extended? But how can extended matter be made up of what is not extended? Or how is motion from place to place possible, since a moving body must always be in some place? Where is a body when it is not in the place it is just leaving and before it is in the place to which it is moving? We do not deny the existence of matter, or of time, or of motion because of these seeming contradictions involved in these various conceptions. That is, we do not deny them unless we are out and out skeptics or pure idealists.

A more serious difficulty connected with freedom, from the theistic point of view, is the reconciliation of freedom with God's foreknowledge. How does God know future free acts, if it is not from a knowledge of the way a man's character is bound to react to particular situations? Or to complicate the problem a little more, how does God know conditionately future free acts?

There has never been any entirely satisfactory philosophic explanation of this. We really do not know how God does foreknow free acts, or conditionately future free acts. It is a mystery, and it will always remain a mystery—until that day when we look out on life freed from the limitations of a space-time world.

The difficulty really comes from our inability to understand the existence of a Being outside of time, to whom there is, properly speaking, no time. To God there is no future and no past. His existence is always one perfect now. Consequently, he does not foreknow; He knows. He does not know acts that are future to Him, but acts that are *present* to Him—although even the word present might be open to question in connection with this Being who exists outside of time. The acts that are future to us, are not future to God.

Properly speaking, then, there is no reason why our acts should be determined in order that we should reconcile God's knowledge of them with their actual performance. We might just as well say that God could not know our past acts, unless they had been determined. But God really knows our past acts in the same way that He knows our future acts—because both are present to him.

This is not simply a mass of words, or an evasion of the difficulty. It is an attempt to bring home the fact that God's kind of existence outside of time is so different from ours in time, that we can draw no conclusion from our own experience. How this can be, is another matter. However, in discussing God's foreknowledge I previously used a few illustrations of the relativists to indicate a line of thought that seems to throw a little light upon the problem. These illustrations do not solve the whole problem, they do not enable us to understand everything about God's knowledge, but they at least indicate that there is a solution. That solution may be far beyond the power of our limited intellects fully to achieve, but we are not therefore justified in denying either human freedom or what, because of our limitations, we call God's foreknowledge. It is possible for us to hold fast to both free will and God's knowledge, confident that the seeming contradiction is merely due to our own limitations.

In fact, I believe it is easier to hold fast to both freedom and God's knowledge by facing frankly the problem in this way, than it is by trying to give an explanation which really does not explain. For quite often the young mind that has been satisfied with the supposed explanation matures sufficiently to realize the inadequateness of the explanation, and then seeks refuge in either determinism or a limitation of God's knowledge. Much better it is for those who believe in freedom and God's knowledge to admit frankly that there is a problem in reconciling the two.

Another difficulty in regard to freedom is sometimes drawn from the field of physics. It has been demonstrated, so runs the argument, that the sum total of energy in the universe remains a constant. It is transformed from one kind of energy to another, but no energy is ever lost or ever created. This is known as the law of the conservation of energy.

Now if this be true, every manifestation of energy must be merely the resultant of previous energy. When I strike a key on a typewriter, I have not added to the sum total of the energy of the universe. But, proceeds the argument, this is only on the assumption that this use of energy is determined by purely physical and chemical laws. If there were such a thing as free will entering into the process, then there would be a creation of energy.

The argument seems to limp somewhat. For

the will might simply act as a sort of prism, rearranging the parallelogram of forces in such a way as to bring about the desired result without either adding to or subtracting from the sum total of physical force in the universe. This was seen even by outstanding physicists, like Lord Kelvin, when the law of the conservation of energy was applied much more rigorously than it seems to be today. And the changed attitude of physicists seems to me to empty the argument of whatever plausibility it used to have. For instance, Millikan says: "The two fundamental principles, conservation of mass and conservation of energy, are now gone *as distinct and separable verities,* as each in itself a universally applicable proposition" (Robert A. Millikan, *Evolution in Science and Religion,* Yale University Press, 1927, p. 46).

And an equally authoritative scientist, A. S. Eddington, in a book only a few months off the press, makes the application to this very question of free will. "In the old conflict between will and predestination," he writes, "it has seemed hitherto that physics comes down heavily on the side of predestination. . . . Here I have set forth the position of physical science on this matter so far as it comes into her territory. It does come into her

[203]

territory, because that which we call human will cannot be entirely dissociated from the consequent motions of the muscles and disturbance of the material world. On the scientific side a new situation has arisen. It is a consequence of the advent of the quantum theory that *physics is no longer pledged to a scheme of deterministic law.* Determinism has dropped out altogether in the latest formulations of theoretical physics" (A. S. Eddington, *The Nature of the Physical World*, Macmillan, 1928, pp. 293, 294).

Again Eddington writes, "The determinism of the physical laws simply reflects the determinism of the method of inference . . . But making all allowance for future progress in developing the scheme, it seems to be flying in the face of obvious fact to pretend that it is all comprehensive. Mr. X. is one of the recalcitrants. When sound waves impinge on his ear, he moves, not in accordance with a mathematical equation involving the physical measure—numbers of the waves, but in accordance with the meaning that those sound-waves are used to convey" (Eddington, *The Nature of the Physical World*, p. 271).

There are serious difficulties, certainly, in regard to free will. But it is only popularizers of science, or men from other fields who have not yet caught up with the leaders in physics, who look upon the law of the conservation of energy as ruling out human freedom. And when all due allowance is made for the difficulties of freedom, the difficulties of determinism seem greater, and the arguments in favor of indeterminism stronger. It is not a mere play on words to say that the more *liberal*-minded view favors the *libertarian.*

VI. IMMORTALITY

Science and the soul; analogies to immortality; difficulties of annihilation; metaphysical proofs of immortality; the nature of the next life.

VI. IMMORTALITY

ALL down the course of history man's written records show that he has been concerned intensely with the problem of survival after death. The Hebrew Scriptures, the Egyptian Book of the Dead, Greek and Roman legends, show glimpses of man's thought about this question of personal immortality. And going back beyond written history, we find in the cave-drawings of pre-historic man, and in his burial remains, indications that even in that remote period he had some beliefs concerning a life after death. While coming to our own day, the growth of spiritism is a significant fact as indicating man's preoccupation, in an age of skepticism, with some empirical proof for an existence beyond the grave.

Next after a belief in some sort of deity, a belief that death does not end all is among the most persistent of man's intellectual conceptions. Different ages and different races have differed widely as to the nature of the life after death, but all have united on the fundamental fact of such a life.

Side by side with this belief, however, there has been a stream of disbelief. Individuals have doubted the fact of survival after death. Skeptics in all ages, for one reason or another, have scoffed at the idea of immortality. And a generation ago, when a mechanistic conception of the universe was commoner than it is today, men who had imbibed a modicum of science used to claim that science had finally done away with the ancient superstition of a soul, and especially of a soul which lived after the death of the body. Everything was thought to be explained by chemistry and physics. And while it seems too crude an attitude for intelligent, educated men, yet it was representative of a fairly large group to say that they had dissected innumerable bodies, and had never yet found a soul! As if an anatomist had ever isolated a pain, either! Yet these same men did not deny the existence of pain.

At one time, I suppose it would not be too much to say, the word "soul" was taboo among many who aspired to be called scientists. For while even then many of the greatest scientists, such as Pasteur, Roentgen, Lord Kelvin, were also devout believers, the general popularization of science was materialistic and mechanistic. Fortunately, however, men of science are no longer afraid to mention the soul. In the epilogue to a recent book (*The New Reformation*, p. 273), Professor Pupin of Columbia writes: "The physical and the spiritual realities supplement each other. They are the two terminals of the same realities; one terminal residing in the human soul, and the other in the things of the external world. Here is one of the fundamental reasons why Science and Religion supplement each other. They are the two pillars of the portal through which the human soul enters the world where divinity resides. This is the mental attitude which dictated these narratives. If the signs of the times do not deceive, then there is a universal drift toward this mental attitude. This drift I call the New Reformation."

Elsewhere Professor Pupin is even more explicit. He tells us that so far from science undermining his belief in immortality, it rather supports and confirms this belief. "Although science does not offer mathematical proof of the immortality of the soul, it gives us plenty of food for thought and belief, plenty of ground for intelligent hope. And it adds to our conviction that our physical life is only a stage in the existence of the soul. In my opinion, all scientific evidence tends to show— not to prove but to point toward the belief—that it is very unlikely that the soul of man is going to cease its existence when the body perishes" (*Literary Digest*, October 1, 1927, p. 33).

Science itself seems to be becoming more and more spiritualized. In fact, I should say that various modern scientific developments make it easier rather than harder to believe in the human soul, and to believe in the persistence of this soul after death. From a biological standpoint, for instance, the teaching of science that man develops from a one-celled organism, instead of doing away with the need of something in addition to the mere chemical elements of that cell to direct its growth, so that the millions upon millions of cells finally arrange themselves in the complicated adult body, rather emphasizes the need of some coördinating influence. Driesch calls it an entelechy, and Pupin a spiritual coördinator. But the name is unimportant. A soul by any other name would mean as much.

And from the standpoint of physics, matter has melted from the solid, stolid, conception of the nineteenth century, until it is almost spiritualized.

Matter has become little more than the points of force of which Boscovitch had an inkling. We do not know as much about matter now as we did fifty years ago—which is equivalent to saying that we know enough now to admit our ignorance. After a lecture in which Professor Millikan had frequently used the word "spirit," a man in the audience asked him quite aggressively to define "spirit." Millikan answered that he would be very glad to, if his questioner would first define matter. The heckler said no more. Physicists are less dogmatic now than were Tindall's contemporaries in their assumption that matter is the only entity. And though we know so little, yet it is easier to conceive of a union between this etherealized matter and spirit than it was to conceive of such a union with the earlier conceptions of matter.

Psychology, too, is coming around to recognize the need of a soul. There is no way of explaining human intelligence and human freedom except on the basis of some non-material part in man which thinks and wills. As Chesterton has said, a caveman could draw a picture of a monkey, but no monkey ever drew a picture of a man; or as Pupin puts it, man worships, the lower animals do not. The power to represent by lines on a flat surface an object of three dimensions requires an abstracting faculty which mere matter cannot account for; the act of worshiping is a spiritual attitude which requires a spiritual power to accomplish.

Of course, all this says nothing specifically about the immortality of the soul. Conceivably there might be a spiritual part of man which ceased to exist when the material body through which it functioned ceased to exist. From the standpoint of philosophy we can never be certain on this point—unless, indeed, there should be in some way communication with those who have died.

Nevertheless, even on the question of the immortality of the soul, modern science helps rather than hinders belief. The theory of evolution, so prevalent in scientific circles today, falls in perfectly with the idea of a life beyond the grave. For if there is evolution from the first one-celled animals up through all the complicated structures that constitute the animal kingdom, to man himself, it seems plausible that the higher part of man should evolve in an environment most suited to itself.

Looked at from this standpoint, death is analogous to the issue of the butterfly from the chrysalis.

It is the beginning of a new existence, as different from the old existence on this earth in the prison house of a material body, as is the existence of the butterfly different from that of the cocoon. As the butterfly is freed from certain limitations placed upon the cocoon, so the soul is freed from certain limitations placed upon it by union with the body. And the fact that very little in our present existence implies such a different mode of living, is no stranger than the fact that nothing in the cocoon predicts the butterfly.

The reasonableness of belief in the life of the soul after death in a very different sort of existence is not at all invalidated by the present dependence of the soul on the body, or on any part of the body. The illustration of the butterfly and the cocoon serves the purpose of bringing this out quite clearly. In the chrysalis state, the butterfly that is to be is shut up in a cell, without power of loco-motion, feeding upon very different food from what it will need in its next stage. Nothing in the nature of the chrysalis would lead us to suppose that this dingy, formless, immovable creature would some fine day change into a brilliantly col-ored, wide-winged, roving animal, sucking its sus-tenance from the nectar of flowers, and vying with them in its beauty. I suppose that one who had known only the chrysalis would scoff at the idea of the butterfly emerging from it. It is acquaintance with the fact which has made it a commonplace for us.

Another example that has been used to show how inconclusive is the argument against immortality from the dependence of the soul on the body, is the condition of a man in a house. In order to see—assuming no artificial light—he must have windows. But no one would conclude that when he leaves the house he cannot see, because he leaves the windows behind him. He can see, because the windows were a condition of seeing only when they were a condition of the light from outside reaching him. When he changes his mode of life so that he has direct contact with the light, he no longer needs the windows.

Just so it would be illogical to conclude that because the soul, while in the body, needs the windows of the eyes in order to gain certain knowledge of objective things, that therefore it cannot get this knowledge when it leaves the eyes behind it in leaving the body. Doubtless, the knowledge it obtains will be different from the knowledge it obtains through the eyes, because that is a sensation dependent upon material conditions, or at least the knowledge will be obtained in a different way. Nevertheless, we ought to be suspicious of the dogmatism that would deny the possibility of knowledge apart from such bodily sensations.

Perhaps a still further illustration of different kinds of existence may bring home more strikingly the possibility of personal immortality. We have all had so far two kinds of existence, about as different from one another as the present existence would be from the future existence that I predicate. The first existence was that of the embryo. It was as intimately dependent upon another as our soul is now dependent upon our body. We were imprisoned in our mother's womb as completely as the soul is now imprisoned in the body. We had no existence apart from her, although we were not she. And nothing in that embryonic existence in the womb, with the blackness of the tomb around us, would ever have led us to suppose that we were preparing for the present life.

Let us suppose that two human embryos in the same womb could think and in some way communicate thought to one another. They know, we imagine for the sake of the argument, their present existence, with all its limitations. One of them, by a daring act of faith, suggests to the other that this embryonic condition is a preparation for a much freer existence in which there will be sensations of sights and sounds of which they can have now no conception. How the other, with what he thinks is a more common sense or scientific attitude, might ridicule such a suggestion! To him what was really birth would be death. There would be nothing beyond the womb, just as to some in this life there is nothing beyond the grave.

II

Naturally, these illustrations are not conclusive proofs. They are merely analogies which may help some to realize that there is nothing inherently absurd in believing that death does not end everything for us. While these analogies help to make immortality more plausible, they really do not prove the existence of the human soul after death. There are, however, stronger arguments, though I must admit that apart from revelation there are no absolutely conclusive proofs of immortality. Immortality cannot be proved in the same way that a proposition in geometry can be proved, in the sense that anyone who understands the premises must grant the conclusion. Without expecting too much, then, we may now give a little time to the consideration of some other arguments for immortality.

With our American practicality, we are likely to judge even religion by results, and to ask of a belief in immortality what good it accomplishes. Now such an attitude is not necessarily to be discountenanced. We have rather high authority for judging trees by their fruits, and we might just as well start by asking what fruit is produced by a belief in immortality.

Well, from a practical standpoint, those who believe in immortality are likely to be better to their neighbors than those who believe that this world ends everything. And since all of us have neighbors, anything that will make them treat us better is of vital concern. If they do not cheat, or steal, or destroy our property, or attack our person—in other words, if they are moral—we stand to profit.

But to be effective, the moral law needs a sanction, whether we look upon that law as merely the mores of social consciousness, or as an objective relationship with the Creator. And certainly the belief in another life, where transgressions of this law will be inevitably punished, and where the

keeping of the moral law will inevitably be re-
warded, is a more effective sanction than a vague
belief that the wages of sin is death even in this
life.

Of course, there are a great many professed believers for whom this sanction of another life is
ineffective. They live as if they had no such
belief. And, on the other hand, there are numbers of professed unbelievers who do keep what
we call the Ten Commandments, although they
attribute no divine sanction to this code. We are,
however, considering the general tendency of belief or unbelief, rather than what happens in excep-
tional cases. The average man with a conviction of
life after death will be a better neighbor to us
than the average man without such a conviction.
Belief in personal immortality is an asset for society. There is a pragmatic value in faith.

A well known unbeliever, it is true, has argued
in just the opposite way. He has maintained that
a man who knows that suffering in this life will
not be made up for in another will treat his suffering neighbors more kindly than one who believes in
a future life. But if I were alone on a raft with a
stronger man whose life here depended upon doing
away with me, I had rather—other things being

equal—take my chance with one who believed in immortality than with one who did not. The conviction that he would be gaining eternal happiness by withholding his hand would be more effective than the thought he was robbing me of the only life I would know—at the same time that he was robbing himself of the same life.

But apart from practical results, a belief in immortality fits in better with science's fundamental conception that this is a reasonable world. That conception implies that everything has not only a cause but a reason. Why, why, why is the constant query of the scientists, as well as how. Yet it should be abundantly clear that this world really has no meaning if everything some day is to end in a grand smash, if all gains, moral and material, will ultimately be lost. It means little that science patiently demonstrates the reign of law, the dominance of cause and effect, in physics and chemistry and astronomy. The whole kit and caboodle is without a reason, unless there is some permanent purpose working through the universe.

All the self-sacrificing researches of scientists who forewent physical comfort to devote themselves to intellectual pursuits would be utter foolishness on the supposition that there is no soul and

[221]

no immortality. We admire these men because we instinctively pay tribute to character. The development of character is the most admirable thing we know. But what would be the use or the reason for developing character at the expense of sensual gratification if the soul is really no higher than the body, if it is destined to the same annihilation? There would be no sound basis for our preferring character to money or the things that money will buy.

Closely allied with this question of character development, is the problem which was troubling the thoughtful long before the Book of Job was written—why the wicked prosper and the righteous suffer.

And certainly we are too sophisticated today to accept the naïve explanation of Job's friends, that when those who seem to us righteous suffer, it is because their righteousness is only seeming. In reality, they said, there is some secret crime which accounts for the suffering. And although as a general thing, the keeping of the Ten Commandments does bring more satisfaction, even in this life, than the breaking of these Commandments, there still remain some outstanding examples of men sacrificing temporal prosperity for the sake of their own standard of virtue. They are true to their ideal of character, and they pay the penalty in this world.

Of course, there is a certain satisfaction for them in this. Virtue, to some extent, is its own reward. Nevertheless, there is a serious problem here, which cannot be solved by any philosophy which makes this world the end-all and the be-all of everything. If there is no future life, in which these inequalities will be made up and removed, then this world is not the reasonable place demanded by science. Life is a huge injustice.

But with the assumption of a future existence for the spiritual part of man, everything falls into its proper place. There is a reason for sacrificing the material and the bodily to the spiritual ideal of character. Somehow, each will get his due. We may not know the mechanism and details by which this will be accomplished, but we can see that such a process is possible.

Without this future existence there is no way of perpetuating the moral gains of mankind. Evolution is empty. Ultimately it must cease. A few billion years more or less do not matter from the philosophical standpoint. A period will sometime be written to all mankind's noblest endeavors.

And without a future life, there is no solid motive on which to base the enthusiasm necessary for social service. The motive for self-sacrifice is withdrawn. All man's altruistic struggle for others collapses. It is true, indeed, that today we have the phenomenon of great numbers of men not affiliated with any church working strenuously for human betterment here and now. But of this great horde, many have a conviction of personal immortality. And of those who have no formal conviction of a life after death, numbers really have some sort of unanalyzed belief. They have not thought through their own position sufficiently to realize how far it is based on belief in the spiritual part of man surviving the grave.

Very, very few men can be thoroughgoing atheists, denying the immortality of the individual, and at the same time earnest workers for social progress. Those few who can combine these attitudes, are no fair sample of what would happen if men generally were robbed of this belief. They are the exceptions. Certainly human relations at present leave much to be desired. There is entirely too much selfishness. But there would be a great deal more selfishness if everyone believed that this world was the only one, if the grave meant complete extinction of the individual.

But let me call your attention to the fact that those who refuse to believe in personal immortality because no convincing argument can be presented to them for that belief, are themselves indulging in belief. If immortality cannot be proved with the absolute convincingness of a proposition in geometry, neither can extinction be proved in the same way. To take the attitude that immortality has not been proved, and therefore to suspend judgment, might, indeed, be logical. But to be dogmatic in the denial of immortality is to fail in the truly scientific spirit.

If no traveler has ever returned from that bourne of the grave to tell us of a life beyond, neither has any returned to tell us that no such life exists. There is, as a matter of fact, considerably less proof of extinction than there is of persistence of life after the grave. All our instincts, all the aspirations of mankind for untold centuries, all the demands of social organization tend in the direction of survival after death.

And if there is a law for the conservation, in some way, of matter, so that the ultimate constituents of matter are never completely annihilated during our experience on the earth—although, of course, all matter is doomed to ultimate annihilation—does it not seem reasonable that no spirit should be annihilated? And if there is a law of the conservation of energy—so that no physical energy is ever completely lost—so much, perhaps, being saved from nineteenth century physics—may we not think it probable that no moral energy is ever lost, that our gains in this direction will be conserved through immortality? The ultimate annihilation of matter in the last great cosmic cataclysm, whatever that may be, does not affect the question. Matter will be annihilated, because of its nature as matter. But the nature of spirit does not prevent the conception of perpetually existing spiritual beings, and we may well ask that a reasonable universe should provide for the immortality of its spiritual entities.

III

Metaphysics is today somewhat out of fashion. Nevertheless, I shall have the temerity of broaching a metaphysical argument with you in order to offer one more proof for personal immortality. And in spite of the unpopularity of metaphysics, I venture to assert that this metaphysical argument for survival is the strongest that we have. Some day, perhaps, metaphysics will come back into its own, and with that revival will come a deeper appreciation of the philosophical arguments for immortality.

At any rate, science, which started out so bravely in separating itself from metaphysics, seems to be getting more and more metaphysical. By its very name, physics proclaims its separation from metaphysics; yet such leading physicists of the present day as Millikan and Pupin are indulging in speculations which are only a very thinly disguised metaphysics. They have gone far beyond—*meta*— the physics of the last century, and have entered metaphysics. Once this is grasped, their example becomes the best apology for the frank presentation of metaphysical arguments in connection with the spiritual survival of man after death.

It was fairly customary among the 1880 model of scientists to claim that everything could be explained by physics and chemistry, using these terms in a narrow materialistic or mechanistic sense. I have referred before to the naïveté of the man who denied the existence of the soul because he had never found a soul with his dissecting knife;

but I may be allowed to refer to it again because it illustrates so perfectly a certain type of mind of the Victorian era. We need to have it emphasized that this attitude was once quite common. But when physicists began to postulate not only atoms, but ions and electrons, men became less sure of nineteenth century infallibility. Scientists knew that there were many things in this universe which they had not seen or touched. They were drawing inferences as to their existence from the effects they did see and touch.

So in regard to the soul of man, philosophers had long inferred the existence of something non-material in man from the non-material human phenomena with which they were familiar. Matter is always made up of parts. The tremendous change in our ideas of matter since the days of Huxley and Tindall still leaves the possession of parts as essential to matter. In man, however, in spite of his material body, we find certain phenomena which cannot be explained except on the supposition of a unifying principle devoid of parts, and consequently non-material or immaterial. The mind of man cannot be matter, because matter is made up of parts, and mental phenomena demand a principle devoid of parts; matter, with its parts, cannot be the utterly simple principle which is the mind of man. As some wag has expressed it, with a greater accuracy, perhaps, than he suspected: "What is mind? No matter. What is matter? Never mind."

The first phenomenon implying an indivisible entity in man is the power of forming abstract or universal ideas. If man's mind were like a material mirror, merely reflecting the sensible objects presented to it, every idea the mind had would correspond to an individual object. I would know Peter, and James, and John. But I should never be able to abstract from the particular characteristics inhering in each, and rise to the conception of man as a species that was neither Peter nor James nor John, but which had whatever was essential to each as a man. If man were merely material, then his ideas would be material, occupying space, and corresponding part by part with the existing object of the ideas. Or it might be more correct to say that if man were wholly material he could not have any ideas at all. He would have only sensible images.

The second phenomenon implying a non-material ego is the power of comparing ideas and forming judgments from them. We can, for instance, affirm that the soul is immortal. The idea of "soul" is pronounced compatible with the idea of "immortality." This is not a process that can conceivably be performed by a purely material being or organ. Comparison of one idea with another is not like the comparison of one triangle with another, by which we superimpose one on the other and conclude that they are equal or symmetrical. A triangle has parts, and we fit corresponding parts against one another. But the idea of "soul" has no extended parts to fit against corresponding parts in the idea "immortal." The idea "soul" is immaterial, having existence only in the conceiving mind. How can a purely material being take such an entity and compare it with an equally immaterial entity, "immortal?" When a camera can measure beauty, or a scale weigh justice, then we may believe that matter can compare the immaterial.

Moreover, if a purely material mind were to make the comparison, what would be the mechanism of the process? If the idea "soul" were in one part of the mind and the idea "immortal" in another part of the mind, how would they ever be brought together for comparison? The ideas could not compare themselves, any more than if they were in two distinct minds. Being separated by parts of the mind, they could have no contact. Nor could a third part of the mind compare them, because it would know nothing about them, since they are in another section of the mind. The only way in which the formation of judgments can be satisfactorily explained is by a mind that has no parts, that is, in metaphysical language, simple, or without composition.

The more complex the mental processes involved, the more clearly they prove that they depend ultimately upon some indivisible entity, which we call the soul. If we go beyond the simple statement "the soul is immortal," and make this conclusion the end of a long chain of reasoning, so much the more do we demand that the agent drawing the conclusion should not be made up of material parts.

Numerous other illustrations of phenomena requiring for their explanation an immaterial agency could readily be given, but I shall content myself with suggesting just one more—the power of reflection. "I" can think of myself, and "I" can think of myself thus thinking of myself. The mind can turn back upon itself, while all the time realizing the complete identity of the "I" that is thinking and the "I" that is thought of. No material thing can do this. A knife cannot cut itself, a brush cannot brush itself. Part of a penknife cannot cut the whole of itself. The whole of an extended body cannot act simultaneously upon the whole of itself, realizing that the complete entity is thus reacting on the whole being. It is impossible to conceive of a material being doing such a thing. And consequently, since the soul can do this very thing, it is not an extended material body made up of parts.

We must go a step farther, however, to show that such an immaterial being would possess immortality. And the way to take this farther step is to analyze the manner in which material things lose their identity. A material object ceases to exist in one of two ways. Either the parts constituting the object separate, as when the legs and back and seat of a chair are taken apart; or the object on which a particular thing depends separates into its component parts, as when a bubble bursts the iridescent colors on its surface disappear.

Now it is clear enough that if a thing has no parts, then it cannot cease to exist by a separation of parts. Consequently, the human soul, not having parts, cannot cease to exist in the first way we have said that material things lose their identity. But there are those who think that the human soul, even if it be immaterial, must cease to exist whenever the material body with which it was united ceases to exist as a living thing. They claim that the soul is like the color on a soap bubble, and when the human body bursts, as it were, the soul can no longer continue to exist any more than the colors can exist without the bubble.

But those who argue in this way overlook one very important fact in regard to the activities of the soul which we have been considering. It is true that these activities are in the life we know dependent upon the body, and especially dependent upon the brain. But that is an accidental dependence. There is nothing in the nature of these mental phenomena which demands such dependence. Since ideas are essentially immaterial in such a way as to require an immaterial agency for their formation, it is conceivable that an immaterial agency might form ideas independently of a material object.

Color, on the other hand, is fundamentally dependent upon matter. The iridescence of the soap bubble is simply the conformation of that film of water so as to refract light in a particular way.

Once that conformation changes by the bursting of the bubble, obviously the light is no longer refracted and reflected. There is nothing about the phenomenon that suggests the immaterial or independence from the material.

IV

The idea of a hierarchy of being is one of the most familiar concepts to scientists. And now and then some very remarkable hypotheses have been based upon this hierarchical idea. For instance, chemists were familiar with certain elements showing for the most part a regular progression in atomic weights. But there were a few lacunæ. The daring suggestion was, therefore, made that these lacunæ were simply due to our ignorance. In reality, so the hypothesis went, the elements existed to fill up these lacunæ, to make the progression actually regular, though at the time we had no experience of these elements. The claim was made that these elements must exist somewhere in the universe, if not on our earth. And the prediction was wonderfully fulfilled. Some of these elements have since been discovered through spectroscopic analysis or in other ways.

Well, a somewhat similar idea can be applied

to the question of the human soul. We know the hierarchy of being ranging from inanimate matter, up through the organic world in its lowest forms of plant life, to sensitive animals which cannot think or will, to man who does think and will. There is progression, development, evolution. Does that progression stop short with the existence of sensitive, intelligent beings wedded inexorably to matter and enjoying a merely temporary existence as individuals? Or does this progression continue through the cycle of our conceptions of the possible, to embrace beings whose cognitive and conative part may somehow exist independently of matter? The philosopher replies affirmatively. And so he expects the existence of man's spiritual part—his soul—independently of man's body after the death of that body. It is a position analogous to the expectation of certain elements existing to fill up the lacunæ in our hierarchy of material existence.

With the limitations placed upon us in this material, space-time world of sense perceptions, we cannot, naturally, know very much about the activities of such an existence. But we can indulge in more or less plausible speculations concerning the kind of life disembodied souls will lead. If there is a survival after death, when the soul is no longer united with a material body, what is the nature of the soul's activities in that state?

First of all, we may readily enough discard certain crude pictures of this life. Golden streets and pearly gates and strumming harps are merely analogous to the diagrams scientists draw of the electronic composition of atoms. No one really claims that they correspond to actuality. They are merely useful illustrations. And with the progress of knowledge their usefulness may cease. In fact, they may become decidedly useless or even hurtful, as obscuring rather than illustrating, the real truth.

When we get down to the bare essentials, all we can assert definitely, from a philosophical standpoint, is that the part of man which now knows and thinks and wills, through the medium of a sensitive body, will in that other state be able to know and think and will in some way without that body. Even in this life we get glimpses of a more direct way of learning than the ordinary one through the senses. We all have our intimations of spirituality. And as in this life, the highest pleasures are not those of the sensitive body, but rather of the knowing and willing soul, so in that

[236]

life we shall be able to enjoy in a much more perfect way these joys of knowing and willing.

We do not now understand the method by which we shall know and love in that other state. But we may presume that certain limitations inherent in a space-time material world will be removed. Here all our knowledge is based upon sense-perceptions. It is an indirect way of knowing, and subject to many inconveniences. When the material senses, however, no longer exist, then the soul must have a more direct way of perceiving truth.

Again, a limitation of this world regards time. We can know only those beings who are living at the same time, and in the same place. In fact, we are restricted still farther, to acquaintance with those in our particular social sphere. The great of the past are beyond our association, and perhaps innumerable kindred souls of the present are debarred by difference of language and geography. In the next world these artificial limitations of time and place and social custom will disappear. There will be but one present. And in some way, all beings will be known to all others.

Finally, we have in this life the limitation of attention. We can attend to only one person at a time. If we are listening to a particular individual, we cannot listen to half a dozen others. But is not that a limitation of our material bodies, rather than of our spiritual minds? May we not imagine that pure spirits will be able to receive communications from innumerable other pure spirits all at once in this indivisible present without one interfering with the other?

Surely all these conceptions of existence hereafter open up tremendous possibilities of happiness. Instead of being the dull and stupid affair that so many persons imagine, heaven—for this is heaven—will be the most active existence possible. There will be much more activity in heaven than there is on earth, because the limitations inseparable from material bodies in a space-time world will have been eliminated. Besides, the highest powers of the soul—intelligence and conation—will be exercised about the First Cause itself, embracing all perfection, summing up all that is beautiful, lovable, desirable.

But if this be heaven, is there also a hell, and if a hell, what is it? Well, just as the exercise of the intellect and will furnish the highest pleasures even in this world, so a frustration of the exercise of these powers spells the greatest torture. Frustration is the depth of suffering. And so we may assume, that in the next life frustration will furnish the keenest suffering to those who have used their faculties in such a way in this world as to be unable to use them properly hereafter. There will be the realization in a much clearer way than is possible here on earth of the infinite loveableness and satisfyingness of God as an object of knowledge and of love, and at the same time, a sense of complete frustration in the attempt to use one's intellect and will towards God.

Who suffers such frustration? Only those who have completely turned away from God as their last end in this world, and who enter into the next world so turned away. Heaven and hell are not so much a place, as they are an attitude of mind and will. Milton puts into the mouth of Satan the words:

> "The mind is its own place, and in itself
> Can make a heaven of hell, a hell of heaven,"

and there is a sense in which these words are true. It is not God Who damns a soul to hell, who sends the soul to some particular place where there are external means of torture, so much as the soul which damns itself by fixing its powers of knowing and loving in such a way as to exclude God, the only object which can satisfy them.

Do any persons so use their faculties in this life, and die with them fixed in this way? No one knows. We have been warned by the Scriptures to judge not, that we may not be judged. But from an intellectual standpoint, the supposition seems justified that happiness in the next life comes from the satisfying exercise of one's highest faculties on the supreme Object of knowledge and love, God; and unhappiness comes from the frustration of this exercise. Each will experience this satisfying exercise, or this frustration, according to the way he has used his faculties here on earth.

We have come, then, to the end of man, and to the end of these talks. I have tried as best I could to show you first of all the great need of spiritual values for your success and happiness even here in this world; and to go on to suggest ways of reconciling the fundamental spiritual truths of religion with the other subjects you are studying at the same time. Civilizations rise and fall, philosophies come and go, scientific theories advance and retreat in the ever shifting scene of human endeavor—but there endures a persistent Credo. Men do not live by bread alone, but by every word of spiritual truth. There will come a time in the life of each one of you when you will be shaken to the depths of your souls. And well it will be for you if then you can fall back upon a deep religious faith, if you can cry out in your agony, "I believe, Lord, help my unbelief." For in that agony religion will be the only source of strength and consolation.

But as a man soweth, so shall he reap. And if in the time of crisis you wish to reap the consolations of faith, you must sow those seeds and cultivate them with all your will. Faith is a moral virtue as well as an intellectual conviction. To appreciate the force of religious arguments, one must try to be religious. Every deliberate sinning against conscience, every failure to live up to the implications of religion in the moral order, is undermining faith. Too often, indeed, a loss of faith is a moral collapse rather than an intellectual process. Men cease to believe, because belief would convict them of sin. They are following the primrose path of dalliance, instead of the heights of a rigid mental discipline.

The will and the intellect are so bound together that no man may completely separate them. And for him whose will is strong to do the right, for him his faith is firm to hold the truth. And so I do not know how better to close these talks on faith than with these words enthroning the power of will:

"O well for him whose will is strong
 He suffers, but he will not suffer long;
 He suffers, but he cannot suffer wrong;
 For him nor moves the loud world's random mock,
 Nor all calamity's hugest waves confound,
 Who seems a promontory of rock,
 That compassed round with turbulent sound;
 In middle ocean meets the shock,
 Tempest buffeted, citadel-crowned."
                    (TENNYSON: "Will.")

INDEX

Absolute, 94
Abstraction, power of, 157 ff.;
  and soul's existence, 229 ff.
Adam, 147
Agnosticism, 11 ff.; and suffering, 11 ff.
Animals, intelligence of, 157 ff.
Atheism, blankness of, 11 ff.,
  111 ff.; difficulties of, 11 ff.,
  47 ff.; and morality, 96 ff.,
  101 ff.; and social service,
  16 ff.; and suffering, 11 ff.
Augustine of Hippo, Saint,
  130, 147

Baptist, John the, 136
Boscovich, Ruggiero, 34, 213
Broadcasting and revelation,
  28 ff.
Butterfly and immortality, 214

Catherine of Genoa, Saint, 130
Causality, principle of, 6, 74,
  82 ff., 118
Characteristics, acquired, 152
Chesterton, G. K., 213
Chrysalis and immortality, 214
Civil law and conscience,
  112 ff.; and morality, 102
Clock and infinite series, 87 ff.
Communion of saints, 32
Conscience and God, 96
Contingent beings, 89 ff.
Contingency, argument from,
  89 ff.
Coöperation of God, 128 ff.
Creation, 48 ff.; process of,
  146 ff.; and design, 71 ff.;

and diffusion of heat, 64 ff.;
  and evolution, 47 ff.; and
  relativity, 60 ff. [126 ff.
Creatures, dependence of,
Credit, a phase of faith, 5
Custom and morality, 97 ff.,
  103 ff.

Darwin, Charles, 149, 152, 153
David, King, 99
Death, 12 ff.
Decalogue, 36 ff.
Design in universe, 71 ff.
Determinism, *see also* Free-
  dom, Free Will, Indeter-
  minism, 164 ff.; inconsisten-
  cy of, 172 ff.; and conscious-
  ness, 189 ff.; and life, 171;
  and morality, 166 ff., 195;
  and pessimism, 167 ff.; and
  reasoning, 169 ff.
Dogmatism of scientists, 144
Draper, J. W., 25
Driesch, Hans, 149, 212
Dunninger, Joseph, 161

Eckhardt, Johann, 130
Eddington, A. S., 203, 204
Einstein, Albert, 60
Energy, conservation of, 202 ff.;
  and free will, 202 ff.
Entelechy, 212
Eternity of God, 118 ff.
Eternity of universe, and evo-
  lution, 47 ff.; and relativity,
  60 ff.; and diffusion of heat,
  64 ff.
Eve, 147

[243]

INDEX

INDEX

[245]

INDEX

Suffering, problem, 132 ff.; value of, 132 ff.

Supernatural and science, 138 ff.

Telepathy and prayer, 139

Theism, difficulties of, 11; and suffering, 12 ff.

Theology and science, 34 ff.

Thomson, Arthur J., 66, 68, 138

Thorndike, Lynn, 26

Time, 120 ff.; immortality, 237 ff.

Unbelievers, conduct of, 18, 106 ff.

Underhill, Evelyn, 130

Universal ideas, 229 ff.

Universe, eternal existence of, 48 ff.; limited, 60 ff.

Visual images, 160 ff.

White, A. D., 25

Whitehead, A. N., 7

Zahm, J. A., 32